The Lawyer's Guide to Legal Process Improvement

EDITED BY LAURA SLATER

Globe Law
and Business

Editor
Laura Slater

Published by
Globe Law and Business Ltd
3 Mylor Close
Horsell
Woking
Surrey GU21 4DD
United Kingdom
Tel: +44 20 3745 4770
www.globelawandbusiness.com

ISBN: 978-1-98358-179-5
A catalogue record for this book is available from the British Library

Contents

Executive summary

"If you can't describe what you are doing as a process, you don't know what you are doing." W. Edwards Deming

OVER THE past decade, law firms and the legal market have changed irrevocably. New service models have invaded traditional law firm territory and new technologies are transforming the practice of law. Clients now have a greater say about how their work is carried out, and they expect law firms to employ the same process improvement techniques they themselves use to reduce costs and improve efficiency and predictability of outcomes.

Respondents to Altman Weil's 2014 Law Firms in Transition survey[1] only expected the internal and external pressures on law firms to increase over the next ten years – yet less than a third said that they were taking steps to address the situation by making their work processes more efficient. For those firms that are embracing process improvement now, this is a huge opportunity to get ahead of the competition. Bringing together the advice, guidance, and expert knowledge of lawyers and consultants with first-hand experience of process improvement in law firms, this report outlines how to devise, implement, and manage an effective legal process improvement strategy.

There are many approaches to process improvement and several are described in this report. Whichever direction a firm takes, it is going to require a considerable culture change, and the first stage of any program must always be to gain firm-wide support. The opening article in this report makes the case for process improvement and provides successful examples of legal process improvement (LPI) in action. Following on from this, the second chapter in the introductory section discusses process improvement as a growing trend amongst law firms and outlines points to consider when to introducing an effective LPI program, from planning through to managing the internal change program.

Legal processes can often seem too complex to break down, yet however many variables there may be, there are common, repeatable steps in all legal work that can be recorded, examined, and improved upon. The second section of the report describes how to build a simple process map that will enable you to understand how the various processes in your organization interrelate, and how they can be managed better, staffed more appropriately, or otherwise improved in order to make them more efficient and cost-effective. The articles that follow introduce several tried-and-tested approaches to process improvement in a law firm environment.

Section three looks at how elements of project management, Lean Six Sigma, and knowledge management can complement and drive a process improvement program. One article describes the define, measure, analyze, improve, control (DMAIC) methodology, which is a core tool in Lean Six Sigma, and the author provides case examples from law firms that have successfully employed both the full DMAIC approach and the accelerated "Kaizen" method to streamline their processes and boost their profits.

While process improvement is about the bigger picture, project management provides the tools to effect change on a matter-by-matter, lawyer-by-lawyer basis, and it will form an integral part of any process improvement strategy. Key topics covered in this section include the relationship between legal project management (LPM) and LPI (and how the former can pave the way for the latter), practical advice on how to implement a simple LPM framework, and the role of LPM in devising a pricing strategy that will both satisfy clients and increase profitability on a matter-by-matter basis.

A firm's KM staff will likely have valuable experience of implementing firm-wide initiatives and they will almost certainly play an important role in any LPM and LPI projects. Therefore, this section also provides guidance on the key points knowledge officers should be aware of when working to implement a successful project management initiative. This is followed by an illuminating case study from the chief knowledge officer at Littler Mendelson, who describes how the firm responded to a client challenge to lower costs by revolutionizing its case management process. The study describes the development and implementation of the firm's case management system, Littler CaseSmart, from the initial process mapping stage, to considering questions of staffing and the technology required, and the lessons the firm learned from the project.

Online services are transforming the legal market; with innovative new service models increasingly meeting client demand for cost-effective, easy-to-access legal advice from a reliable source, traditional law firms that have not yet embraced online services are at risk of losing ground to more forward-thinking competition. The final section of this report considers how firms can take advantage of the opportunities offered by online portals to meet the needs of the modern client while also reducing costs. Accompanied by case examples, it covers the various types of online delivery available and describes how to establish and implement an effective online strategy.

Today's clients don't just want to know what work the firm has carried out on their behalf, they also want to know *how* that work was completed. By mapping, analyzing, and then optimizing their processes, law firms will be able to assure their clients of greater predictability and efficiency and, ultimately, better value while also significantly improving their own bottom line.

Reference

1. Altman Weil, 2014 Law Firms in Transition: An Altman Weil Flash Survey, see www.altmanweil.com/dir_docs/resource/f68236ab-d51f-4d81-8172-96e8d47387e3_document.pdf.

PART ONE

Introduction

The case for process improvement: A Lean Six Sigma perspective

By Catherine Alman MacDonagh, CEO and founder, Legal Lean Six Sigma Institute

Most processes fall far short of their potential

What Lean Sigma practitioners often find is that the processes people think are in place do not really exist. Or we find that each person has his or her own process. Or that the processes take much longer than people believe. As Henry Ford famously said, "Most people spend more time and energy going around problems than in trying to solve them." What we see in law firms is that most people are spending more time and energy in solving problems created by ineffective processes than in trying to improve them.

In many cases, we have seen that what started out as a fairly decent practice has changed considerably over the years. Usually, this is due to well-intentioned workers who employ "workarounds" in order to compensate for the failure of the process to support the person working with it. The result is that law firm processes often, by lack of attention or intention, wind up looking like New England farmhouses: built in a random fashion; tacking on one thing after another as the years pass by; and producing a result that looks nothing like what one would have designed if the architect had started to draft the plans with the current requirements in mind.

Those who have employed Lean and/or Six Sigma will attest to the fact that, as soon as we start to describe and measure a process, we will begin to see things that could be improved, either in the client's eyes or the eyes of the firm/department – or both.

In fact, most of our processes fall far short of their potential and improving them will benefit *both* the client and the firm/department. The reality is that if we continue to operate our processes as we always have while expectations of clients, owners, regulators, etc. rise, we will inevitably experience a performance gap. However, if we improve our processes before those expectations rise, we will develop significant advantages.

Understanding changing client expectations

The other thing we will do when we begin to learn about and engage in process improvement is demonstrate our ability to speak our client's language. As Karen Dalton and John Dugga observe, "While lawyers generally know their clients well, they are often surprised at how much their clients know about Lean, Six Sigma, project management, and even agile. Clients expect exceptional legal expertise, but what they are most interested in is how the firm is going to do their work. Clients are very interested and receptive to innovative value-added services that deliver results."[1]

DuPont believes that legal professionals should bear some responsibility for their client's bottom-line success and that legal services, no less than other services, can improve through process analysis. They say process improvement is for lawyers who "are driven by a commitment to continuous improvement and who recognize that the complete lawyer brings more to the table than legal acumen".[2]

As, to be cost-effective, work must be done by the lowest cost resource that is capable of performing it, process improvement and project management becomes critical. Detailed knowledge of the effort required to carry out the work is required, recording time very important, analyzing past engagements is key, according to David Hargis, chief operating officer at Tucker Ellis & West, who suggests that "metrics shift from the billable hour, and that new capabilities are required – profitability methodology, reward systems".

With that in mind, it would be difficult to reasonably argue the point that process efficiency and ongoing improvement in any professional services work is a bad thing. Yet for years the legal profession has managed business in a manner that creates disincentives to do so. The billable hour is one such distinguishing riptide. Thompson Hine is an example of one firm that has established a clear and structured path to keep the focus on delivering what the client wants in the way the client wants it, rather than anchoring on historic ways of undertaking client work.

"Our clients tell us regularly, through our formal surveys, our client Summit, and ongoing discussions that great work is more than just understanding the legal discipline. It is as much about how that work is delivered. Great work demands excellence in how it is outlined, staffed, monitored, and managed, with diligent communication from beginning to post-close. General industry has understood this philosophy for years. We have the benefit of that roadmap to apply within our firm – and we have invested the time and resources to get it right", says Sue Brelus, chief marketing officer at Thompson Hine.

Thompson Hine's director of legal project management, Bill Garcia, notes examples where the rigor of comprehensive legal project management has enabled the firm to increase efficiency and meet very short timelines under tight budget constraints: "Client needs vary based on the matter. This process forces the upfront discussion that puts a clear spotlight on what is valued most in the particular situation. Agreement on what defines success, followed by carefully outlined process, monitoring the process, reporting to identify issues, and continuous communication empower firms to optimize service delivery. Without all the pieces, process may be improved, but it will not be optimized", remarks Garcia. "The LPM conversation between client and outside counsel forces self-examination, which leads to improvement."

Convincing lawyers to embrace Lean Sigma and project management is no small undertaking. In fact, both the change management and the work of process improvement itself require vision, commitment, serious discipline, and proper allocation of resources. However, we must accept the fact that most lawyers, either by training or nature (or both) seem to approach even the notion of change with a large dose of skepticism. We seem to challenge everything and base our thinking and decisions on precedent, rather than the possibilities and benefits that innovation may deliver to them.

Moreover, many lawyers initially resist the notion that their work can be reduced to a series of steps where predictability of activity and budgets are possible. It is important to recognize that their concerns have some merit. Lean Sigma will not work for everything. However, lawyers are fairly quick to recognize how many legal processes have standardized components – such as completing forms or obtaining follow-up information that, when streamlined, can improve the work product produced and the service delivered to the client. In addition, the rising number of Lean Sigma successes is too significant to ignore. The issue is no longer whether Lean Six Sigma should be considered, it is when and how.

From the client's perspective, it is inconsistent to be told that a firm has decades of deep experience in handling a particular kind of matter and then, in the next breath, have it explained that there is no possible way to predict how long something should take, what could happen at each step, and how much it will cost.

Tim Corcoran, a former CEO, considers this home truth on his *Business of Law Blog*, in a post addressing recent decisions regarding, among other things, the use of "principle" or "officer" by the Texas State bar that has justifiably raised industry-wide objections.

Corcoran writes that "Business clients are unhappy. Lawyers in the mid-size and big firms that serve us often do a terrible job of communicating. They fail to properly manage expectations by limiting the client's surprise. They tend to treat each matter as if it's unique and infinitely variable, yet at the same time expect us to believe their experience in a given field is meaningful. They believe in charging higher fees based on the length of time they've practiced, even when they are unable or unwilling to demonstrate this experience by using matter budgets or project plans. And their fees are typically established irrespective of the value I place on the services rendered, and what alternatives exist for me to obtain these same services elsewhere, assuming that the seniority of the lawyer and the time necessary to deliver the work are the primary drivers of value. They claim that non-lawyers in a law firm, or worse, non-lawyers providing legal services outside the structure of a law firm, e.g., an LPO, must be incapable of providing quality legal services, even when these alternative providers can unassailably demonstrate higher quality at a lower cost."[3]

The profession is changing

In their September 2012 *Legal Intelligencer* article, Kristin Sudholz (the first chief value officer in any law firm) of Drinker Biddle and Reath LLP and Jennifer Smuts state it bluntly: "Over the last few years, law firms have blamed trends, the economy and even competitors for forcing them to change the way they run their businesses. Ultimately, it doesn't matter where the blame lies – the profession is changing."

Now that clients are frequently presented with alternative options for getting work done rapidly and at greater value, pricing pressures are increasing, and discussion of different fee arrangements is becoming the norm rather than the alternative, we need good processes more than ever. It is essential to determine what clients find valuable in a process, select the lowest cost resource capable of handling each task in the process every time, and then do and deliver the work with the highest standards of quality every time and profitably over all.

As consultants Adam Smith Esq. succinctly put it:

"We [the legal profession are] being squeezed on the top line:

- by clients exercising pricing pressure and
- by the increasing visibility and acceptability of 'substitutes' for at least some of what BigLaw has traditionally done.

We have overcapacity, as an industry, on the order of 7% of our headcount:

- Citi Private Bank has estimated that if all of the 70,000+ lawyers in their sample of firms were working as many hours per year as they did five years ago, 5,000 of them would not be needed
- Yet we continue not only to prevent attrition from taking its natural course, but we are *adding* to [the] headcount.

Expense growth has again begun to outpace revenue growth:

- Our #1 time-tested technique for increasing revenue is to raise rates; we can do that until the cows come home, but clients will take it right back in decreased realization – now at an all-time historic low for the industry
- Our #2 time-tested technique for increasing revenue is to load up on lateral partners; but in this environment they may be adding more to expense than to revenue.

We are completely unserious about taking the shortest route between two points in terms of attacking both overcapacity and expense growth in a single stroke: We have not even begun to address our equity partner headcount.

- Evidently we lack a sense of urgency
- The tepid, 'no longer in free fall' economy has become the *enabling economy*, coyly inviting us to postpone for tomorrow what no longer seems a matter of great urgency today.
- We have, in short, committed the classic and so-oft-repeated sin of wasting a crisis."[4]

Attitude is a choice. So, I encourage firms to view these increased pressures and changes as opportunities to seize: let's not waste a good crisis! There is no better time than now to embrace process improvement. At this point, conversations about this very subject have become much more commonplace between law firms and their clients. It is not just critical for law firms to be able to talk about why process improvement is important to them and what they are doing to build process improvement capability, it can also serve as a significant way to build and enhance relationships. It differentiates a law firm in the marketplace.

The risks are greater than the challenges

Some are skeptical about the ability of law firm management to adapt and lead their organizations through the changes that are going to be required for survival. I have had the repeated good fortune to work with many managing partners, practice group leaders, and business professionals who have embraced process improvement. What I have seen is that their firms do not just "adopt and adapt"; they also develop high-functioning teams, and significant competitive advantages.

Making the necessary changes will not be easy. As Ray Worthy Campbell explains in a 2012 article for the *New York University Journal of Law and Business*, "The business literature on innovation, which has been largely ignored by scholars addressing legal markets, helps make many things clear. Successful incumbents cannot easily change their business model; their resources processes and values are optimized to their current clients and will resist change. Incumbents can use radical new technologies to sustain their business model, but tend to leave alone new technologies or business processes that do not enhance their offerings to their current clients."[5]

However, the risks associated with standing still, while competitors (even those who have yet to appear on the scene) move forward, will be far greater than the challenges firms will inevitably face in embracing process improvement. "Disruptive entrants can enter the low end of the market with new technologies or business processes, and disrupt the market through a sequence that sees them improving their offerings in an iterative manner, eventually allowing them to challenge for the incumbent's best customers." [6]

The pressure to deliver value

A 2014 research report commissioned by Allen & Overy describes how general counsel are responding to external and internal pressures to change the way legal work is delivered – a trend that has picked up significantly since A&O's last survey, two years before: "Since then, the pace of change has accelerated. 86% of the respondents to our latest survey say they are under pressure to deliver more value to their business for less cost. Many legal teams now face increased workloads with headcount and budgets that are cut or frozen. This pressure is forcing legal teams to explore more fundamental change."[7]

General counsel of "one multinational conglomerate", cited in this latest Allen & Overy report, puts the situation for law firms quite simply: "The firms that sit around and think they are going to be able to just continue doing what they have done for the last 100 years are going to become redundant… The model of the provision of legal services is being challenged now more than ever. Law firms have to constantly think about how they are going to innovate and evolve."

As the report notes, "Not all law firms will be able to rise to this challenge, but it is clear that failure to do so carries the risk of not keeping pace with changing client expectations."

These changing expectations include the requirement that firms provide a "one stop shop" for legal services (39 percent of interviewees); 53 percent of respondents in the A&O survey said they "find it challenging to coordinate different types of legal service providers efficiently". Taking heed of the research, the firm reported, "We are deploying technology, business process and project management to combine traditional law firm services and new legal services into hybrid legal solutions."

Gaining buy-in for process improvement

There is no doubt that it is compelling and even inspiring to learn about who is employing process improvement and project management, and how and where those firms and law departments have been successful. Another key point that helps to make the case for Lean Six Sigma is to highlight the fact that one of our goals in fundamentally changing our processes is to create even greater opportunities for lawyers to focus on the areas where they contribute the highest value, which are practicing law and applying strategic thinking to legal problems. This takes advantage of their experience and training by removing waste by reducing time spent on administrative tasks that irritate them and other non-value-adding activities. It is critical to show that when we improve processes lawyers will still have plenty of latitude and flexibility, since we never gratuitously standardize any part of a process or crudely suggest that improving efficiency is as simple as reducing headcount.

This is especially important where business professionals who are not practicing lawyers are responsible for leading the charge (notice that we DO NOT use the term "non-lawyer"). The practice of referring to professional staff by what they do *not* do is not just one of the unique and negative aspects of the legal profession; it is also, arguably, a violation of the Lean Sigma principle to align and empower employees.

UK-based law firm, asb law, which has offices in Crawley, Sussex, and Maidstone, Kent, provides an example where all employees are integrated. According to its mission statement, the firm seeks "to continuously improve our internal processes so that we operate efficiently and, ultimately, make cost, resource and time savings". In order to facilitate the goal of continuous improvement, "Everyone at asb law is encouraged to challenge the established way of doing things and to suggest improvements. Lean Champions from each team help to coordinate and share ideas across the firm, and lean targets are written into performance measures."

Through this, the firm asserts that "over recent years, we've become quite adept at improving the efficiency and cost-effectiveness of our operations. Our employees are actively involved in questioning not only how we work internally, but also how our clients and suppliers might improve their services. Indeed, we're collaborating with several business clients to help them apply lean techniques to manage risk."

"Working collaboratively also demonstrates congruent beliefs and a commitment to responding to client feedback", says Amy Hrehovcik of Ailey Advisors. She points to the 2014 ACC Survey, which reports that 89 percent of chief legal officers recognize the importance of professional development in advancing non-legal skills among their staff. The non-legal skills most sought after include business management (62 percent), project management (54 percent), and communication (49 percent).

Additionally, early success is important for beginning to build momentum and achieving "buy in" for the initiative as a whole. It is a truism that no organization has a second chance to do something right the first time, so selecting the right baseline or demonstration project that will serve as your firm's own case study will always provide the most convincing evidence that "Lean Sigma works here".

Linking quality and performance

Lawyers, and rightfully so, care a great deal about quality, and often express concern that it will be sacrificed by making a process more efficient. They also worry that profitability will suffer. "One of the first solid pieces of evidence linking quality and business results was groundbreaking research performed by PIMS (Profit Impact of Market Strategy). Over a period of years PIMS amassed a large database documenting the strategies and financial results of more than 450 companies and nearly 3,000 business units in order to study the general relationships between strategy and company performance. Its purpose was not to prove a link between quality and profitability (or between any other particular business strategy and firm performance), but rather to discover those strategic principles most strongly related to performance. Among all the strategic principles distilled from the PIMS studies, one linkage between strategy and performance stood out above all the rest: quality.

A quality edge boosts performance in the short run by allowing the firm to charge premium prices and in the long run by enabling growth of the firm through both market expansion and gains in market share. PIMS found that businesses offering superior product/service quality are more profitable than those with inferior quality, based on two key measurements: return on sales and return on investment. In addition to these profitability and growth advantages, PIMS also revealed other benefits of superior perceived quality: "stronger customer loyalty, more repeat purchases, less vulnerability to price wars, and lower marketing costs".[8]

In short, focusing on quality can help make a very compelling case for trying process improvement. Lean Sigma has provided particularly good quality case studies. This is due to the framework of process improvement and a focus on delivering bottom-line results.

Technology and process improvement

As might be expected, technology is in and of itself a sort of process improvement. When there is an upgrade on a device, for example, it usually presents us with a better way of doing something. These days, we are alerted to upgrades to all our applications with such frequency that it is now common to, quite literally, wake up to process improvement.

While technology is nearly always a part of the solution to improving a process, to a process improvement practitioner, technology alone may often appear to be a solution looking for a problem. It really depends on how we frame what we are trying to solve. For example, if we describe the situation as "we don't have a CRM system", then the only response to the problem is to select, install, and roll out a new kind of technology – a client relationship management (CRM) system. If, instead, we take a process improvement approach and characterize our problem as "we are not capturing firm experience, which is impacting our ability to compete for new work, engage in client development activities, and manage our business processes such as firm mailings", we start to think about all the elements – in addition to technologies like CRM – that will help us address the problem and seize attendant opportunities.

In an opinion piece in *Managing Partner* magazine entitled "Efficiency – your starter for 10", Simon Slater, managing director of First Counsel Consulting Limited and a founding member of the Legal Practice Group, wrote that "The legal service reforms will pave the way for new entrants to the market and competition the likes of which law firms have not yet seen. For many firms the key to survival in the new legal landscape will be investment in efficiency, but where exactly should that investment be made?"

Slater highlighted a small, progressive law firm: "'A single key decision we made recently will be the difference between survival and failure,' said the [firm's] managing partner... His board's decision was to invest no less than £400,000 in technology to streamline its processes and improve the delivery of legal services. When probed, he said the firm could only succeed by becoming truly efficient. Intelligent deployment of technology was the key."

Therefore, Slater advises that firms "Use the right technology to support the streamlining of processes in the delivery of legal advice and client services. Don't over-engineer and recognise that all services commoditise in time... Support the increased dependence on technology with an investment in training for your people. Help them embrace change and new working practices positively." When it comes to Lean Six Sigma, Slater advises firms to "adopt [the] thinking without the dogma. Six Sigma is simply a process used to identify and eradicate defects in manufacturing... On a smaller scale, the same philosophy can be adapted to precedents, knowledge and legal processes... Think about lean management. Law firms are fundamentally simple businesses, but they are often over-managed. Keep management small and 'local'. Consider partial outsourcing, but with care. Control directly what you must. The key test? Is the value people add greater than the paper they push?"

The rate of change is not slowing down. So, if your processes are not changing as fast as the environment is changing, as former General Electric CEO Jack Welch would say, "the end is in sight". The changes in the business environment create ever greater requirements for higher process capabilities and higher process efficiencies. We have extremely talented and capable people working in law firms in all sorts of positions. But they are working with processes that do not allow them to function to their highest levels. Instead, legal and business professionals in law firms are sometimes coping with processes that are horribly broken; at the Legal Lean Sigma Institute, we routinely suggest that when you put talented people up against a broken process, the process will always win.

So, talent acquisition and retention, competitors, technology, employees, regulations, and, most importantly, clients are all part of the driving forces that are creating widening performance gaps in the processes in law firms. Because our processes are not capable, errors are made and waste occurs. Then, we spend time addressing those mistakes, making corrections, pacifying people, and recovering. As a result, it is difficult for anyone to have the time to improve anything. We call this being stuck in the "fire-fighting doom loop".

For law firms, the two most compelling drivers for process improvement are clients and the competition (other firms and legal service providers). We leverage the realizations associated with those drivers to convince law firms of the importance of "pulling the car over and finally fixing the engine rather than continuing to drive or attempting to repair it as we speed down the highway". Process improvement is an excellent way to get out of this "doom loop".

The DuPont Legal Model

In terms of clients driving these changes, Dupont is the most widely known and highly regarded legal department driving efficiency via the DuPont Legal Model, now 22 years old. Dupont's website states that:

"Part of the success of the DuPont Legal Model is its ability to embrace change and adapt to new challenges. In order to continually integrate new strategies and solutions into the DuPont Legal Model, DuPont Legal, its Primary Law Firms (PLFs) and Primary Service Providers (PSPs) have devoted considerable time and money to applying the Six Sigma methodology to processes within the legal department's realm. Six Sigma provides a disciplined approach to business improvement by systematically improving processes and eliminating defects, which are defined as units that are not members of the intended population.

Six Sigma at DuPont Legal has led to savings, process accountability and much more. At the outset, there was little experience in the business world for Six Sigma in legal services. The drive for collaboration and bottom line savings in the Legal Model served as an important grounding.

Within DuPont Legal, early projects addressed:

- Litigation costs
- Patents and trademarks
- Administrative services

- Information technology implementation
- Records management

Six Sigma supports the unique role that the Legal Function provides in its delivery of legal services to the corporation. Aligning with the accomplishment of short- and long-term strategic goals, the Legal Six Sigma adds:

- Support for process excellence in core legal processes
- Adherence to cost effective Control Plans
- The opportunity to identify and lead cross functional projects
- The management of legal risks of the corporation

Today, every global member of DuPont Legal and every PLF and PSP plays a part in Six Sigma. It is the way work is done at DuPont Legal and key to meeting the company's 'Sustainable Growth' productivity goal. Given the Legal Network members' central role in cost savings and risk management, their continued and active involvement is critical to the program's success."[9]

Clients expect efficient processes

Today, many clients' requests for proposals (RFPs) and information ask firms to describe their process improvement or process management programs. RFPs seem to be increasingly focused on understanding how law firms are becoming more efficient – and how the firms suggest, given their knowledge of Lean and Six Sigma, that the clients themselves can be more efficient.

To be clear, today's clients not only expect their law firms to understand and employ process improvement methodologies in their own work, they also expect them to provide recommendations as to how they can help the client in the same vein. This requires that the lawyers and business professionals in law firms – whether they are client facing or not – be able to identify and propose ideas for improvements. Without the language and tools of Lean and Six Sigma deployed on a more institutional basis, this becomes increasingly more difficult, particularly as the work, services, and number and depth of relationships grows between firm and client.

Here are just a few examples from RFPs:

- Please address how you will accomplish greater efficiencies. For example, do you employ project management techniques such as Six Sigma or Lean?
- How and why should Company A have confidence that your firm will handle matters efficiently and in a cost-effective manner without sacrificing quality?
- What changes could Company A implement to make your work for us more cost-efficient?
- Company A seeks reliable, financially stable Law Firms that can meet stringent cost, quality, and service requirements. A team will evaluate each proposal based on various criteria, including, but not limited to... processes generating operational efficiencies.

When competing these days, using smoke and mirrors to respond to specific questions about how your firm is approaching efficiency and employing Lean and Six Sigma will not only be ineffective, but could potentially harm your firm's position and reputation.

These days, there is an increasing need to "get legal procurement's attention", according to Dr. Silvia Hodges Silverstein,[10] whose research and work in procurement is setting the standard.

"Procurement is now involved in the purchasing of legal services and it's quickly becoming the 'new normal.' Larger corporations in particular engage procurement, not only for sourcing low-end, routine or commoditized legal services, but increasingly for higher-stakes legal work as well. But that doesn't mean that law firms or in-house legal and procurement teams are well equipped to deal with this new landscape and to make these new relationships successful."

"Legal procurement analyzes many things that might not have been given a lot of attention in the legal profession before: Industry benchmarking analysis is conducted by 71 percent of respondents in the survey, followed by rate increase analysis and invoice audits (67 percent each). Half of the respondents forecast budgets, followed by alternative fee arrangement analysis, and key performance indicator analysis.

Procurement also embraces legal spend management (75 percent) and e-billing (71 percent). Contract database for legal, matter management and in-house e-discovery are used by 40 to 50 percent of respondents in the survey. Firms' project management and process improvement capabilities are increasingly important: 48 percent of respondents in the survey deemed them 'very important,' another 16 percent as 'important.'"

Uptake of Lean Six Sigma in law firms

David Skinner, a certified Lean Six Sigma Sensei with over 20 years of experience of practicing law in law firms and as in-house counsel in Canada and overseas suggests: "It may be that firms in the UK and Australia are slightly ahead of the curve because they've already adapted business structures that are more conducive to a business-like approach. Let's face it: a huge partnership is hard to manage. If you have to get 900 partners in ten different cities in six countries around the world on board, it's going to take you a while. Smaller firms are more agile and more able to adapt and that's where we see a huge uptake."[11]

With that in mind, it is interesting to read a survey from several years ago that is available from Altman Weil and which includes data on the use of Six Sigma by US law firms. The study found that:

- Three firms or 5.1 percent, had utilized Six Sigma;
- Five firms or 8.5 percent had not used Six Sigma but planned to in the future;
- 51 firms, or 86.4 percent, had not used Six Sigma and had no plans to do so.[12]

Originally developed by Motorola, Six Sigma's value has been proven in companies such as AlliedSignal, Sony, General Electric, Lockheed Martin, Boeing, Verizon, and IBM, just to name a few. Given the success already achieved by many (client) companies as well as law firms who had by now implemented Lean Six Sigma and reported great results, I was astonished that more had not yet utilized the methodology. Things began to change very soon, however.

By September 2008, Seyfarth Shaw, with their emphasis on branding the firm based on experience and results, became a driving force behind change at firms competing against them for clients.

When Altman Weil released their 2014 survey, the contrast to the 2008 responses was dramatic:

"More than 90% of firm leaders have said they believe there is a permanent market shift requiring greater efficiency in the delivery of legal services.

- In the area of efficient legal service delivery, 54% of the large firm group was pursuing change, compared to 34% of the smaller firms;
- 43% of firms offer PM training;
- Only 30% of law firms have taken on the really challenging task of re-engineering work processes."[13]

With 70 percent of firms not yet reporting that they have had the either the interest or the fortitude to employ process improvement, there is still plenty of room in the marketplace for those who are interested in beginning to explore this now – and it is a wise idea to do so while it remains an option, not a requirement. Often, it is the risk and cost associated with not doing something that can provide the most compelling reason to act. Consider this: according to an American Bar Association study released in 2012, 30 percent of legal malpractice suits were the result of administrative errors, including failure to calendar or react to calendar items, and lost files, documents, or evidence. What would happen if your firm decides to do nothing about efficiency?

"As there is a relationship between cost and price, there exists a relationship between process and cost. How a firm performs services impacts cost. Performance is indelibly tied to process/workflow. This is true even in the practice of law."[14] With all of the internal and external pressures to be more efficient and a keen interest from partners in remaining profitable, it is certain that a specific role that is focused on process improvement will become another business function in a law firm that is the rule rather than the exception. The increased number of those responsible for process improvement, project management, and/or pricing suggests that this will occur sooner rather than later.

Award-winning examples of process improvement in action

One of the drivers causing increasing interest in Lean and Six Sigma by law firms is the significant marketing and business development opportunities, along with competition and award-winning ideas, programs, and innovations from other law firms. Examples include the following:

Baker Donelson

One of the first firms in the US to invest in the development of its own legal project management (LPM) system, Baker Donelson received ILTA'S 2012 Distinguished Peer Award for outstanding achievements in the category of "Project of the Year".

The firm states that its system "is an industry leading and patent pending system which can be implemented in any type of engagement – business or litigation... Baker Donelson also formed a Legal Project Management Office (LPMO) to provide support for the BakerManage system and guide the implementation of project management principles across the Firm... The goals of BakerManage include: Evaluate legal processes across the Firm to create guidelines for attorneys which promote consistency, encourage appropriate resource assignment, omit duplication and streamline delivery."

The Hunoval Law Firm

Based in Charlotte, North Carolina, the foreclosure firm was one of five finalists for the "Best Process Improvement Project" at the 15th annual PEX awards, along with Capital One and Pitney Bowes (the winner). Hunoval, a firm set up from scratch in 2009, was nominated for its implementation of Six Sigma principles in a legal environment. According to Hunoval, "this is not about change in how we practice law. It's about law practice management, improving the business side–an idea that is changing how law firms can be run."

What is more, these are changes that appeal directly to how clients run their own businesses: "When they hear us speaking that same language," Hunoval says, "I can see the lightbulb moment where the client or potential client says, 'Oh my God, here's a lawyer who actually gets it.'"[15]

Littler's CaseSmart program

Littler's CaseSmart program has been recognized for creating an efficient and novel way of approaching equal employment opportunity (EEO) and employment litigation work, redesigning the processes to eliminate inefficiencies and inconsistencies. According to the firm's website, "Littler CaseSmart was developed by legal practice management professionals and tenured employment lawyers, all focused on innovation for the purpose of controlling costs and delivering real client value." The firm's innovative approach won a 2012 College of Law Practice Management InnovAction award and a 2011 ILTA "Project of the Year" award. The firm already has a solid track record of experience with CaseSmart, having "successfully handled more than 9,000 charges within the Littler CaseSmart model".

The real innovation that came from carefully and thoroughly mapping out their processes for these kinds of work allowed Littler to develop software that automates and tracks entire processes, which provides their clients with a privileged and sophisticated view of all matters. Littler points out that "The client dashboard provides matter-level data across an entire set of matters, including the ability to filter by type of charge, type of case, location, date range, status, response type, and other criteria. The client dashboard also allows users to drill into specific matters and to view all substantive documents, matter summaries, and intake data. Moreover, your company's preferences for communication protocols, frequency and types of reporting are configurable in the Littler CaseSmart solution."

Seyfarth Shaw

SeyfarthLean has been the subject of numerous articles and representatives from the firm have delivered a multitude of programs and published pieces concerning their broad-based, leading approach to process improvement. In 2011 International Legal Technology Association recognized the firm twice with the Innovative Law Firm of the Year award and Innovative Project of the Year award. The following year, Seyfarth received the College of Law Practice Management's InnovAction Award.

The marketing opportunities that a focus on process improvement generates are significant. Seyfarth Shaw branded its approach "Seyfarth*Lean*", developing a serious competitive advantage and generating a high-visibility campaign around its message about using Lean Six Sigma and project management to drive value for clients. This was a firm that embraced the idea of being first, rather than waiting to see who else would follow, thereby raising the bar for all law firms (whether or not they were pursuing the same clients).

The firm designed a marketing campaign around its work and skill sets that continues to be very effective. Thus, Seyfarth uses the competitive advantages that Lean and Six Sigma can deliver very well. With a program to develop deep skills and projects across the firm, they had real results to include in their award applications, branding, marketing, communications, and business development efforts. As such, they were way ahead of the market and became known for their leadership in efficiency.

Squire Sanders

The firm was recognized in *Law Technology News* in 2012 with the "Most Innovative Use of Technology in a Large Law Firm" award for their Intelligent Discovery Process™, an e-discovery project management and technology platform that leverages disciplined management, predictive coding, and other technology to improve efficiencies in the e-discovery process. The *Law Technology News* award distinguishes Squire Sanders as a leader in the convergence of technology and the law and recognizes its practical application to provide clients with more efficient, cost-effective, and defensible results.

The firm's press materials state that "Squire Sanders was early to recognize the potential of predictive coding and technology assisted review processes. 'We're not just talking about predictive coding, we're using it as part of a disciplined process to deliver better, more cost efficient and defensible results to our clients,' said Scott A. Kane, Chair of Squire Sanders eDiscovery & Data Management Practice. 'Our investment in the Squire Sanders Intelligent Discovery Process™ has paid off not only in terms of client review costs, but also in terms of quality, strategic decision-making and budgeting accuracy.'"

Foley & Lardner

Another approach law firms are taking is to take direct part in a client's own process improvement activities. Nowhere are there greater opportunities to do this than in firms with manufacturing clients.

A supreme example is provided by Foley & Lardner, which was recognized by the Legal Marketing Association (LMA) with the 2014 Your Honor Award in Practice Development. The award recognized the firm's launch of the Legal Innovation Hub℠ for NextGen manufacturers, a firm-wide business development and marketing program devoted to next-generation manufacturing. The hub is comprised of a dedicated network of departments, industry teams, and practice groups and helps manufacturing clients engage in dialogues and tackle the transformational issues associated with next-generation manufacturing.

"Foley has been serving U.S. manufacturers for nearly 175 years, and this is an industry we know well", said Janis Nordstrom, Foley's global chief business strategies officer. "As a result of this program, we are strengthening our reputation as the 'go-to firm' for next-gen manufacturers, helping them collaborate on the legal and business challenges presented by the convergence of technology and manufacturing."

About the author

Catherine Alman MacDonagh, JD is a Legal Lean Sigma Black Belt and a certified Six Sigma Green Belt. A former corporate counsel, Catherine is well known for her thought leadership and successes as a law firm executive. Now a highly rated speaker and consultant, she works with professional services firms to create competitive advantages and organizational transformation through the development, planning, and implementation of innovative strategies, process improvement projects, and business development training and coaching programs.

Catherine is an adjunct faculty at Suffolk Law School and at George Washington University (Master's in Law Firm Management). She is also the chief enthusiasm officer of The Legal Mocktail, an experiential networking training program, and has her own consulting practice, FIRM Guidance. She is a co-founder of the Legal Sales and Service Organization. In addition to *Lean Six Sigma for Law Firms*, Catherine is co-author of two books: *The Woman Lawyer's Rainmaking Game* and *The Law Firm Associate's Guide to Personal Marketing and Selling Skills*.

Please contact Catherine at Catherine@LegalLeanSigma.com, (+001) 857 272 5695, and on Twitter @cathmacdonagh.

This first appeared as Chapter 2 in Alman MacDonagh, C., Lean Six Sigma for Law Firms, *Ark Group, 2014.*

References

1. Dalton, K. and Dugga, J. "Lean and agile: How legal project management can transform client services", *Managing Partner* online, 25 March 2013.
2. Sager, T. L., and Winkelman, S. L., "Six Sigma: Positioning for Competitive Advantage", ACCA Docket 19 (No. 1), 2001.
3. Corcoran, T. B. "Bar Associations: Protecting Consumers or the Status Quo?" blog post, *Corcoran's Law Biz Blog*, 2 July 2014; see www.law.com/sites/jdsupra/2014/07/09/bar-associations-protecting-consumers-or-the-status-quo/?slreturn=20140622111226.
4. Adam Smith Esq., The Enabling Economy: The Essay published 26 August 2013; see www.adamsmithesq.com/2013/08/the-enabling-economy-the-essay/?single.
5. Campbell, R. W., "Rethinking Regulation and Innovation in the U.S. Legal Services Market", *New York University Journal of Law & Business*, vol. 9, no. 1, Fall 2012; www.nyujlb.org/wp-content/uploads/nyb_9-1-1_scissored.7-76.pdf.
6. Ibid.
7. Allen & Overy Global Survey, "Unbundling a market: The appetite for new legal services models", May 2014; see www.allenovery.com/SiteCollectionDocuments/global-survey-lsm.pdf.
8. Ryan, J. "Making the Case for Economic Quality, a White Paper for The American Society for Quality (ASQ)"; see http://asq.org/economic-case.
9. See www.dupontlegalmodel.com.
10. Silverstein, S.H "Get legal procurement's attention" blog post, 19 May 2014; see www.silviahodges.com/?P=1615.
11. Skinner, D. and Skinner, K., "Who says there's no messing with lawyers?", Process Excellence Network, 9 March, 2013; see www.processexcellencenetwork.com/lean-six-sigma-business-transformation/articles/who-says-there-s-no-messing-with-lawyers.
12. Altman Weil Inc, "Results Altman Weil 2005 Survey of Major Law Firm Management Techniques"; see www.altmanweil.com/dir_docs/resource/b9ca8e17-6530-446d-bb8d-62a2376c4602_document.pdf.
13. Altman Weil Inc, "2014 Law Firms in Transition An Altman Weil Flash Survey; see www.altmanweil.com/dir_docs/resource/f68236ab-d51f-4d81-8172-96e8d47387e3_document.pdf.
14. Kubicki, J., and Wood, C. "Business Design for Law Firms, Part 2", Commentary on Legal Transformation Institute online, 3 July 2014; see http://legaltransformationinstitute.com/blog/2014/7/3/business-design-for-law-firms-part-2.
15. Carter, T., Foreclosure firm goes statistical to improve speed and quality, *American Bar Association Journal* online, see www.abajournal.com/magazine/article/foreclosure_firm_goes_statistical_to_improve_speed_and_quality.

Dissecting processes: How to create a legal process improvement program

By Kim R. Craig, global director, legal project management office, and Andrew M. Baker, global director, legal technology innovations office, Seyfarth Shaw

THE PRACTICE of law is a process. It may be an incredibly complex process with a large number of variables, but it is a process. The complexity of some legal work can skew practitioners' views of what they do, causing them to see the law largely as an art, rather than having some relation to science.

Nevertheless, the general mindset in law firms has started to change over the past few years. Clients are focused on how legal work is going to be done. Processes are relevant. As a result, a few law firms are taking this process-centric view of the practice of law very seriously. Flowing from that evolved view of legal work, firms are beginning to implement legal process improvement (LPI) programs.

This article examines the growing trend of LPI within law firms and discusses how to introduce an effective LPI program. It outlines how LPI can support other strategic foci, how to assess your firm's legal processes, what to consider when planning for LPI, and how to manage the internal change program.

Understanding processes

LPI involves the systematic review of current legal processes and then optimizing those processes to achieve a desired end state. The impact of LPI is real, especially from the client's perspective. LPI brings enhanced efficiency, consistency of experience, predictability in spend, and transparency to the attorney-client relationship.

The first key step is understanding the current state of a specific legal process. This requires sitting down with your legal teams and getting a handle on a specific scope of the work. Ask yourselves questions like:

- What tasks make up this type of work?
- Who handles those tasks?
- What precedential materials and tools are used in a given task?
- How much time is necessary to execute a specific task?
- What decisions do we have to make?

It all needs to be catalogued and made digestible for those who are not experts in the area.

At Seyfarth Shaw, this is done through process mapping exercises. First, a particular piece of legal work is pinpointed for the purpose of determining and capturing best practices. A team of approximately four to eight subject matter experts at all levels – partners, associates, paralegals, and administrative assistants – is selected.

One person is then chosen to lead the mapping session. This needs to be someone who is an excellent facilitator, can engage participants at all levels and drive a team of highly-skilled professionals who typically have very strong opinions to reach consensus on the most efficient and effective means for delivering the legal work.

As the team determines the appropriate-

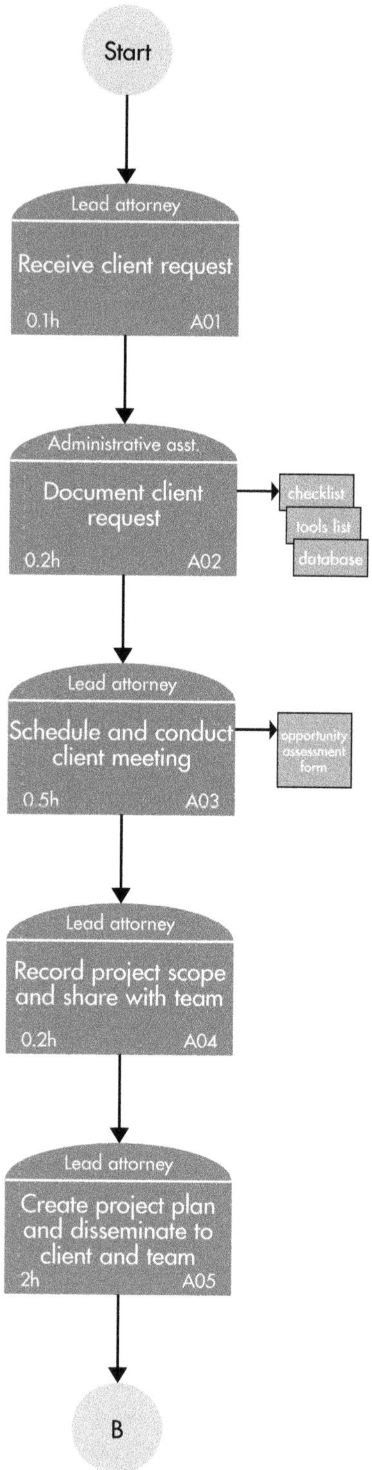

Figure 1: Sample excerpt from legal process map

level timekeeper to be assigned to each task, it also estimates how long each task should take to complete. This is done by leveraging historical data and balancing it with the practical experience of the legal teams. Though each matter brings unique challenges, this approach improves our ability to plan for future engagements (see Figure 1).

If you've never done this before with a group of attorneys, it's an interesting activity that yields many beneficial outcomes. The banter alone between attorneys on how best to complete a given type of work can make process mapping worthwhile.

Once you understand your process, you can begin to improve it. The analysis around that review is fairly straightforward. For instance, you will want to:

- Determine whether unnecessary rework is being done;
- Identify work that can be "pushed down" to lower-cost resources without sacrificing quality; and
- Look for opportunities to inject technology to increase efficiency.

But, you will need a documented process to conduct this review.

Process mapping sessions provide a forum for knowledge sharing. In short order, each participant gains a sense of ownership in designing a process and develops a focus on efficiency and continuous improvement. The team will identify "best in class" templates and sample documents that can be made accessible to clients and the legal team.

The investment and effort of the process mapping team is captured electronically and shared with others who deliver similar legal work. Most importantly, it is displayed graphically, making the process and its attributes easy to digest. The final map represents the collective knowledge of seasoned experts and is valuable as a training tool for novice legal team members.

No single person can master all substantive areas in which large or mid-sized law firms practice. It is because of that breadth in process that technologists, knowledge management professionals, and others labor to provide solutions with precision. But, they may miss the context in which their solutions can be deployed.

A documented process changes the game. The organization at large can better provide value to specific practices when a documented process is in hand. The lateral thinking and creative solutions generated by these maps can "wow" attorneys and, most importantly, their clients. However, a documented process is necessary for that problem-solving to occur.

Supporting other strategic foci

Over the past five years, a slew of acronyms have come into focus for law firm management. The alphabet soup has become fairly thick.

For instance, the use of legal project management (LPM), legal process outsourcing (LPO), alternative fee arrangements (AFAs), knowledge management (KM), and business intelligence (BI) have trended up since the economy took a nosedive. LPI can now be squarely added to the mix.

At a macro level, there is much overlap between these areas. However, LPI may be the most powerful. It is the glue that binds other disciplines and brings forth the synergies that management teams seek.

LPM

The planning portion of LPM can be the most challenging aspect of the discipline. Work will often come in the door with immense pressure, and the amount of time available to plan a matter can be limited.

Furthermore, in-depth preliminary planning isn't part of traditional attorneys' genetic makeup. They rely on expertise and years of experience to do their work. Having processes memorialized and at the ready provides the right jumping-off point for the creation of project plans. Each process will have to be tailored to a given engagement and client need, but that starting point makes all the difference.

LPO

Price pressures within the industry have resulted in a greater exploration of the outsourcing market. Properly outsourcing legal work is a challenge for a number of reasons. Aside from the ethics, quality, and logistics involved, it can be difficult to determine what the partnering organization should do and how. Having a documented process, however, provides a framework for that discussion and for subsequent action.

AFAs

Be it via fixed fees, success fees, or portfolio pricing, law firms are carrying additional financial risks when executing legal work. Proper pricing is important to landing deals, and the methods of execution are proving crucial to ensuring profitability.

Understanding your process enables you to price services more accurately and helps to ensure you are doing work in a manner that best positions your firm to end up on the right side of the ledger.

KM

The focus of knowledge management groups varies, sometimes greatly, from firm to firm. Generally speaking, KM has had success tackling very broad problems, but groups sometimes falter in targeting specific areas of practice. It can be difficult to pinpoint and select the right projects, to formulate approaches, and then figure out how best to execute them. However, within a process-centric legal environment, KM teams can better implement powerful solutions that are narrowly tailored to a specific practice. A documented process brings these specialists closer to the legal work.

BI

Like companies in virtually every industry, law firms are working to become more data-driven. However, getting data, formulating baselines, and setting benchmarks for comparison are a challenge. LPI creates a basis for this. If matters are generally approached the same way and properly tracked, we can discern trends and patterns and make better business decisions.

Introducing LPI internally

Process improvement has a place within all law firms. However, only a handful of firms have made serious inroads. But, as they say, the journey begins with a single step.

First, recognize that this effort is fraught with change management hurdles. You'll want to attack the problem from the top and bottom. You'll need a champion or small team of attorney champions to help push efforts from above. They will need to be able to voice the rationale for the efforts and aid in the bending of ears.

Next, you'll need a boots-on-the-ground tactician. This person will help to coordinate the process capture efforts and facilitate a knowledge transfer from legal teams. There are many disciplines from which you can pull talent, but Six Sigma, Lean, and total quality management are a few notable methodologies.

The number of people with legal context in these areas is small so, if you do not have a resource on staff, you will likely have to reach outside of the legal vertical. If you go that route, you will need to find someone with flexibility in approach. Out of the gate, none of these approaches will work in a wholesale, formal manner.

After you have your "drivers" and "doers", you will need to target your first area for process improvement. Making that determination is not easy and there are a few key factors to weigh (see box: Getting started with process improvement).

All change requires an element of "sales". You are going to need someone who can articulate – in terms legal teams understand – what this effort brings and how important it is. It needs to be persuasive.

With most attorneys, the client angle will need to be a key thread in your story. Altruistic messages touting the broad firm impact may not garner much appreciation – at least at first. The effort needs to be real to your participants – real situations, real impact, and real goals.

However, as with all things, those leading the effort will need to properly set expectations. No documented process will be perfect. As you capture processes, you will have to be cognizant of the level at which you operate.

If you come in too high, the output will not be helpful and the value will be lost upon your constituents. On the flipside, fly too low at first and the process capture can be too daunting and time-consuming.

Taking it to the next level

Once you have your process improvement program up and running, you will then be primed to set your sights on more advanced goals. There is an almost unlimited number of directions that your organization can take, but two large challenges should be on your radar early in your journey:

1. The ability to institutionalize your processes; and

2. Whether you can provide transparency to your clients.

Seyfarth Shaw has been systematically capturing and improving legal processes for over six years through its SeyfarthLean program. Institutionalizing a process-focused approach to legal work has taken significant effort. There is no silver bullet.

Changing culture is hard, and simply throwing money at the problem does not move the needle much. It was only through broad attorney and staff trainings, small group awareness sessions, and targeted one-on-one sessions that we were able to get penetration within the organization. And, at all points, we routed positive client feedback to the broader organization for inspiration and reinforcement.

While fighting the cultural battle, we also developed a number of custom, technical solutions to provide transparency to clients. We abhor the idea of the black box. Through an elegant combination of extranets, financial reporting, and matter management, we provide a means for clients to stay apprised of our processes and progress.

Further, these systems underpin our legal teams' approaches and enhance the consistency of the client experience. We have made great headway and we have more creative solutions on the horizon.

In surveying different industries, it's the overlap of distinct disciplines that is proving to be exciting and powerful. The examples are numerous and include:

- Statistics and graphic design (data visualization);
- Computer science and biology (bioinformatics); and
- Physical exercise and technology (personal metrics).

Will the crossroads of law and process engineering be the next multidisciplinary domain to take off? Some firms are betting that it will, and it's a bet that's already paying off.

Getting started with process improvement

- **Frequency** – How often do you do that type of work? The more frequently your firm does the work, the more value it will garner from its efforts.
- **Complexity** – Your first foray into process improvement may not be the right time to tackle the most arduous area of work your firm undertakes. Cut your teeth on an area that isn't dizzyingly complex.
- **Currency** – Are there areas of work that are hot right now and for which you are experiencing increased requests?
- **Client partnerships** – Do you have a client that has particular interest in process improvement? You may consider it a partner on your legal process improvement work and focus on a type of work you handle for it.
- **Pain points** – Is there a type of work that is less profitable than desired but that you want to maintain for strategic reasons? Imbuing process rigor here may help to increase margins and make this work more attractive.
- **Involved experts** – The personalities of the experts involved in your first project will be supremely important. To one extent or another, all lawyers are driven by precedent. As such, many can be apprehensive about being a test subject. Ensure it's a receptive party. And, make sure they know that they're about to be your Project Mercury – not a guinea pig.

A version of this article appeared in Managing Partner *magazine in May 2012.*

About the authors

As global director of Seyfarth's Legal Project Management Office, Kim Craig leads the industry's largest legal project management program in the world. As client-facing business partners, the Legal Project Management Office drives the efficient delivery of legal services by applying their expertise in agile project management and process improvement to enhance the client experience. Their partnership with Seyfarth's Legal Technology Innovations Office positions the LPMO to identify and assemble architected business solutions for the firm's clients.

Kim is an active leader in driving the firm's distinctive client service model – SeyfarthLean® – a combination of Lean Six Sigma, innovative technologies, knowledge management, alternative fee structures, continuous improvement, and project management. She has co-developed the curriculum and delivery of the firm's SeyfarthLean Yellow Belt program and is a member of the firm's SeyfarthLean Steering Committee. In 2011 she was the recipient of the International Legal Technology Association's (ILTA) Professional Services Champion of the Year Award for her leadership in legal project management. She is an active member of the Project Management Institute and is working in collaboration with the American Bar Association to develop a project management curriculum for legal practitioners.

As global director of Seyfarth's Legal Technology Innovations Office, Andrew Baker is focused on enhancing the delivery of the firm's legal services through the use of technology, knowledge management, process improvement, business analysis, and project management. In this role, he oversees a team of legal solutions architects who anticipate, identify, design, and drive innovative business solutions. As an attorney and a technologist, Andrew regularly provides technology consultation to clients and firm attorneys. He is a proven innovator and has overseen the completion of dozens of complex legal technology projects.

Andrew is a member of the firm's SeyfarthLean® Steering Committee. Seyfarth's commitment to delivering legal services in a new way – with emphasis on value and continuous improvement – has been praised by the Association of Corporate Counsel as being "five years ahead of every other AmLaw 200 firm". Andrew currently serves on the International Legal Technology Association's (ILTA) Knowledge Management Peer Group Steering Committee.

PART TWO

Process improvement approaches

Mastering complexity: Current and future tools for legal process optimization

By Tim Hanson and Simon Thompson, directors, Change Harbour, and Robert Millard, partner, Møller PSF Group

LEGAL PROCESSES extend across offices and practice areas. Aligning and optimizing them (to say nothing of integrating them) can be very difficult, not least because of the human element. This is perhaps why some of the recently emerged global law firms appear to be "kicking the can down the road" on this rather than tackling these issues decisively. But tackle them they must, if they are to service their clients in the seamless, global way that they claim they can. So, too, must other medium to large-sized law firms.

In this article, we focus on processes specifically in the practice – those that drive the development of legal work product and its delivery to clients. This article is not about legal project management, although that (and sourcing) are crucial aspects of process efficiency and good matter management generally. Nor is it about "disruptive innovations" (a badly misused term) that radically reinvent processes. Rather, it is about law firms developing a deep understanding of the legal processes in their practice so that they can be better managed and, where appropriate, improved.

An overview of the benefits that can be achieved through this are outlined in Figure 1 (overleaf). At stake, at the highest level of abstraction, is enhanced competitive advantage, more valuable client relationships, and greater efficiency – all of which translate directly into improved economic performance.

Legal process workflows

Modeling legal processes is not a new idea. The concept is well known to anybody that has done any kind of legal knowledge management. Legal project management is a basic first step. It does not make much sense to talk of redesigning processes if one does not have the basic disciplines in place.

How does one go about that, though? Is it possible to model legal processes through workflow studies in the same way that one can for business processes? Usually not. Processes involved in the practice of law are fundamentally different to those involved in the business of law.

Addressing legal processes through workflow techniques is fatally flawed in three ways:

1. It attempts to apply linear thinking to an area that is adaptive and dynamic. Legal transactions are not linear and don't obey consistent rules.
2. The number of variables involved in all but the simplest transactions quickly lead to process flow diagrams and models that are too complex to be useful.
3. The restrictions that they place on lawyers stultify them and, worse, can prevent them from delivering the most appropriate solutions to their clients.

The 18th century British philosopher and jurist

Value	Outcome
Become more efficient	Improve gearing
	More effective re-use of knowledge
	Manage portfolio of work
Get better return on investments	Better training of lawyers
	Improve returns on investments in KM
Manage operations and risk	More consistent adherence to best practice
	Audit of risk management decisions
	Management of changing legal and commercial consideration
Collaborate	Work more effectively within the organization
	Work more effectively with business partners
Create new products	Create effective knowledge and training products quickly
	Create new commoditized products for clients quickly
Transform a practice	Model legal processes
	Idenfity mature, developing, and high-performing areas
	Streamline and apply best practices

Figure 1: The benefits to be derived from understanding and improving legal processes

Jeremy Bentham once wrote "the power of the lawyer is in the uncertainty of the law". Even beyond that, each kind of matter has its own specific set of characteristics including rules, legal risks, commercial risks, types of roles, templates, and statutory tasks. Many matters bridge several different types of transaction, meaning that multiple sets of characteristics apply. For instance:

- A lawyer is instructed to purchase a commercial property in London (triggering the set of characteristics associated with commercial real estate in London); but
- The transaction requires funds to be raised by selling assets in Germany (triggering a second set of characteristics); and
- By issuing shares or borrowing funds in Paris (triggering a third set of characteristics).

For an experienced lawyer, this level of intellectual complexity is handled with ease. For a process modeler, reducing all of the possible permutations of this transaction to a process flow diagram is diabolical in its complexity.

Some large global law firms have wasted a great deal of time and money in trying to map out "standard" transactions. These have collapsed as soon as even moderate levels of complexity were introduced – not least because the technology used has been inadequate beyond the simplest "vanilla" transactions.

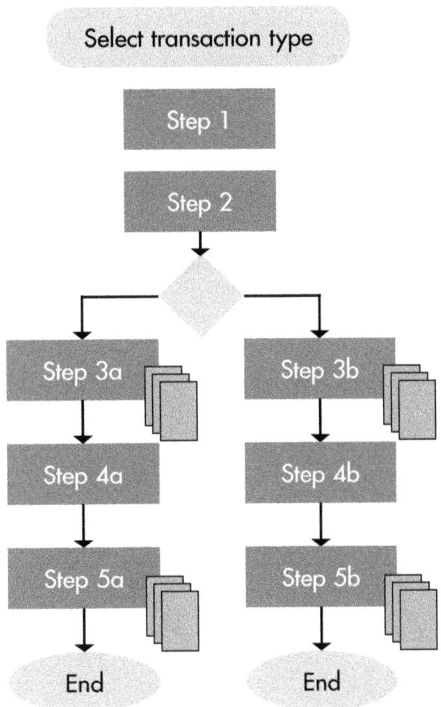

Figure 2: A generic workflow diagram of a simple legal process

Future disruptive technology

One development that would constitute a game-changer (a "disruptive innovation" in the true sense of the term) in legal process management would be the significant introduction of artificial intelligence (AI) into legal knowledge management.

Some of the global IT companies serving the legal profession are working on this already, although a useable product is probably still some years away. Two parallels from outside the legal profession illustrate the potential.

1. Rapid and intelligent scanning of big data for relevant content

In 2011, the IBM computer "Watson" competed against and beat two former winners of the TV game show *Jeopardy*. Watson had access to 200 million pages of structured and unstructured content, but was not connected to the internet.

The software that powered this feat is now being advanced to, upon verbal query, examine millions of pages of medical textbooks, journals, and other references in order to diagnose and propose treatment for, theoretically, every known human ailment.

How might this concept be applied to the practice of law? Imagine a resource that could quickly scan millions of pages of legal references, across multiple languages, in response to simple verbal cues, and quickly deliver intelligent responses that comprehensively address the matter.

2. Unstructured prompts and "pushing" knowledge to lawyers

In current knowledge management systems, lawyers must search for the knowledge they need. Imagine if that knowledge could be "pushed" to them instead. Examples that already exist in other industries include iTunes and Amazon ("you have previously purchased 'X' so perhaps you would be interested in 'Y'" or "others who bought 'X' were also interested in 'Y'").

A system that "pushed" information to lawyers might suggest the following:

- "You are purchasing a company, so you might want to use 'X' and 'Y' templates."
- "You are financing the purchase by raising bonds in France and Brazil, so you might like to review how we did that

before. Also, 'X' and 'Y' are the lawyers that we have previously used in Paris and Sao Paulo."
- "50 percent of the bonds you are issuing will be sold in Madagascar, so you might like to know the risks associated with that, which are 'X', 'Y', and 'Z'."

Lawyers would be presented not with directions but rather options as they constructed transactions. They would then be able to use their own skill and judgment to decide how best to proceed.

Such a system would also evolve and grow as it adapted to every decision that each lawyer took, constantly improving its ability to push out ever-more relevant options.

Tools for the present

For now, we don't have such tools. However, one can better understand legal processes and how to improve them by segregating them into three types:

1. **Collaboration processes** – These facilitate lawyers collaborating together on a matter. They are especially important if the firm has multiple offices or operates a virtual business model (even partially, such as with a significant "work from home" component);
2. **Work product processes** – These actually create work product and deliver it to clients, from matter opening to closure; and
3. **Knowledge management processes** – These collect knowledge, codify it, and deliver it back to lawyers when it is needed on subsequent matters.

Of course, these three categories are not mutually exclusive, but in them lie several things that law firms can do, here and now, to make a start towards improving their legal processes (see box).

Improving legal processes

1. Collaboration processes

- Root out behavior that encourages predatory behavior amongst lawyers. This may require revisiting the firm's performance measurement and compensation systems.
- Find ways to improve IT and other systems, especially across geographies, to drive collaboration (not just referrals) on matters.
- Develop cross-office teams that meet regularly, either face-to-face or virtually, to discuss better ways to collaborate and serve clients together.

2. Work product processes

- Develop dialogues about disaggregating different kinds of legal services into their component tasks and about what kinds of variations typically emerge. It is futile to try to map these out generically into standardized workflow diagrams, but do plan and map out individual matters (i.e. implement legal project management). Matter by matter, make proactive decisions about the best way to source and approach the work.
- Explore billing models that do not involve churning out time for money. Fixed fees create incentives for lawyers to find efficiencies that reduce the transactional cost of a service

because the additional margin translates directly into profit. Churning out billable hours is a real and significant disincentive to this.

- Engage with clients' legal teams to get their views on how the processes involved in serving them could be made more efficient.
- Embrace the inherent complexity of legal services. Do not try to make things simpler than they are. Rather, understand what the key drivers of a matter are and what the key rules are that define a successful outcome – then focus on those.

3. Knowledge management processes

- Keep abreast of the latest developments in knowledge management, especially emerging technologies driven by social media and, in time, artificial intelligence.
- Improve channels of communication between those with experience and those who are learning the ropes. Until "push" technologies become a reality, this is a far more efficient way of accelerating a transaction than wasting hours looking for knowledge. A recent Forrester study found that 45 percent of lawyers spend four hours a week or more searching for content. It also found that a single division of a large UK-based global manufacturer determined that a one percent efficiency increase in their knowledge workers finding information would lead to annual saving of £1.5 million.

A version of this article appeared in Managing Partner *magazine in April 2013.*

About the authors

Tim Hanson is a director of Change Harbour. He has been involved with innovation and change projects within the legal industry since 1997. His particular expertise lies in the exploitation of process, technology, and sourcing to help lawyers execute their work more effectively. This has included developing LPM programs for international firms, lawyer/client process improvement programs, creating and managing numerous change portfolios to meet strategic objectives, and delivering business facing change projects covering matter management, risk and compliance, KM, productivity and collaboration.

Prior to joining Change Harbour, Tim spent 14 years with Linklaters where he was responsible for managing the delivery of the business consulting service for the global practice; helping lawyers to execute matters more effectively though the application of strategic sourcing strategies; aligning the IT strategy to the strategic drivers of the firm; developing and exploiting the investment in SAP to manage business process; and delivering a consulting service to the firm's major clients.

Simon Thompson is a director of Change Harbour. He utilizes his extensive experience in leading edge law firm management, enabling firms to implement innovative solutions to deliver operational effectiveness and support revenue growth. Simon's main areas of focus include organizational design, process improvement, and the alignment of firm-wide systems and structures with business strategy. This involves business and legal management systems across all functions. Simon has particular experience in integrating systems and structures following law firm mergers, to optimize efficiencies and align them with the strategy of the combined firm.

Prior to becoming a consultant in 2011, Simon joined Linklaters LLP in 1994, becoming director of ISS in 2001. Simon developed Linklaters' information systems technology, organization, and governance strategy, leading to the true globalization of IT services across the firm. Between 2001 and 2003 Simon led a global/firm-wide implementation of SAP ("Programme Armstrong") encompassing finance, practice management, client relationship management, and human resources. This was the first full implementation of SAP within the legal industry.

In April 2007, he was appointed global chief operating officer, responsible for leading all of Linklaters' business services worldwide. As a member of the firm's executive committee, Simon was responsible for setting business services' strategy and coordinating all of its activities (HR, finance, IT, knowledge management, risk, marketing, strategy, operations), therefore playing a major role in ensuring that Linklaters' firm-wide strategy was successfully implemented. As Global COO, Simon initiated an ongoing program of change aimed at achieving globalization of services, increased innovation, greater cost effectiveness, and improved quality.

Robert Millard is a partner with the Møller PSF Group and co-head of the firm's strategy practice. At the time of writing the article, Rob was a partner at Venturis Consulting Group. He is also formerly senior strategy manager at Linklaters, and he has practiced as a strategy and management consultant to law firms since 2001. His clients span the globe and, besides law firms, also include some financial services firms.

Besides his consulting practice, Rob also serves as senior vice-chair of the IBA's Law Firm Management Committee and as co-chair of the International Law Practice Management Forum of the ABA Section of International Law. He is co-liaison of ABA International to the Law Practice Division and serves on the advisory board of ABA International's Africa Committee.

Building a simple process map of your organization

By Chris Bull, executive director, Kingsmead Square

ALL ORGANIZATIONS have processes including all legal organizations. Lawyers can have "pockets of excellence" within their business, where processes are defined, documented, and regularly improved. However, the majority of processes in the organization are not. This is a common situation for most legal organizations.

One of the first jobs for firms wanting take a process-oriented view of their business is to understand what processes exist and to get an idea of where they begin, end, and overlap. This involves constructing some form of enterprise-wide process view. This could be in the form of a process map or model (or to the tech-savvy, a process architecture). I will use "map" as my preferred term for the toolkit. The end goal is a single process map that represents what the firm does.

Use a process reference model

Beginning the process of putting all of your firm's activities and functions into a comprehensive process map can be daunting. But there is no need to start from a zero base, as a huge amount of work has been done globally on developing generic and industry-specific models, typically referred to as process reference models.

These standard models do not take away the fundamental task of engaging with the main stakeholders, adopting a common language, and customizing any model to the firm. But it can save a lot of time and enable those putting the model together to ensure their output is comprehensive and well structured.

US-based company APQC is a member-based non-profit organization specializing in benchmarking, knowledge management, measurement, and process improvement. Over three decades, it has developed into one of the most widely recognized and used sources of reference models, evolving what it describes as: "The global language of processes". The company offers a taxonomy of business processes called Process Classification Framework[SM] (PCF) to allow organizations to objectively track and compare their performance internally and externally with other industry-wide organizations. Developed in the early 1990s, PCF began as a tool to support performance improvement projects, evolving into the broad taxonomy that it is today. For more detail on process mapping, visit APQC's website: www.apqc.org.

The electronic discovery reference model

Note that many lawyers have some engagement with a process reference model already – through the electronic discovery reference model (EDRM). Many larger law firms and in-house legal departments will also engage with the IT infrastructure library (ITIL) derived model now used in many IT departments. But an enterprise-wide legal business model is something we still have to work on.

For now, the popular APQC PCF model can be adapted for law firms at a high level without difficulty. Table 1 suggests how a firm's activities can be broken down. The 12 categories at the top of the PCF are fairly broad.

Operating process category		Notes on further breakdown for legal business
1	Develop vision and strategy	■ Divide into enterprise, market/sector, practice components ■ Focus on strategy to build client base and resources
2	Develop and manage services	■ Development of new legal products and service ■ Acquisition of new services (through hires, merger) ■ Development and packaging of know-how
3	Market and sell services	■ Firm marketing and communications ■ Sector, practice, and discipline marketing activity ■ New business development (including pitch/tender) ■ Existing client development
Core processes		
4	Deliver services	■ Service line and practice group specific ■ Matter management processes ■ Document production processes
5	Manage client service	■ Quality and risk ■ Client satisfaction ■ Client relationship management
Supporting process category		
6	Develop and manage human capital	■ HR ■ Recruitment ■ Learning and development
7	Manage information technology	■ IT infrastructure design and maintenance ■ Software development and management ■ IT services
8	Manage financial resources	■ Funding and treasury ■ Engagement to cash (matter financial management) ■ Procure to pay (payables management) ■ Accounting and tax compliance
9	Acquire and manage property	■ Estate management (acquire, manage) ■ Facilities management
10	Manage environment, health and safety	■ Compliance and risk management ■ Environment impact management
11	Manage external relationships	■ Government relationships ■ Regulatory and professional relationships ■ Community relationships
12	Manage knowledge, improvement, change	■ Knowledge development and distribution ■ Continuous (and process) improvement ■ Internal communication ■ Program and project management

Table 1: A comprehensive legal process map.

This first appeared as Tool 1 in Bull, C., The Legal Process Improvement Toolkit, *Ark Group 2012.*

About the author

Chris Bull is a founding executive director of professional services consultancy Kingsmead Square. His consulting career stretches back to the mid-90s, when his focus was large financial services change projects as part of Ernst & Young's market-leading consulting team. The last two and a half years have been spent advising a wide range of professional service firms, with an emphasis on the legal market, on operational change and business management.

Chris is a regular speaker and writer on all aspects of the management of professional firms. His speaking, writing, and advisory work draws on a long track record of senior roles in the sector. As well as spells with Price Waterhouse and Ernst & Young, Chris was a member of the leadership team of law firm Osborne Clarke as the firm expanded rapidly and built a strong market position amongst the best UK firms. His roles there included chief executive, chief operating officer, and finance director over a hugely enjoyable 12-year period. As chief operating officer for Europe and the Americas at professional services outsourcing firm Integreon, he led the development of a legal and business process outsourcing offering that created a legal market leader.

Kingsmead Square was founded in 2013 by Chris and former-Barclays executive Louise Fleming. The firm has rapidly built an impressive client base of some of the most innovative and fast-growing professional service firms and new entrants to the market, including a roster of the most high profile alternative business structures and a number of large law firms.

Chris lives on the slopes of the Mendip Hills in Somerset in the south west of England. He "enjoys" running there and wherever he finds himself on his constant travels, and spends most of his spare time chasing around after his two children.

5S

By Chris Bull, executive director, Kingsmead Square

5S IS a simple and highly practical approach to quality improvement. Traditionally used in manufacturing companies, the emphasis is on a safe, clean, organized workplace and on engaging everyone in the business at the frontline in process improvement. With an emphasis on the physical and visual, 5S can initially appear to be of little relevance for office and service environments such as law firms. However, the principles can be effective in service organizations if applied with care, and there are three main reasons for looking to use this aspect of Lean in legal environments, where process maturity is in its early stages:

- The down to earth practicality of 5S appeals to a wide range of individuals, who can grasp the basic principles and how to apply them very quickly, without some of the cynicism other methodologies can attract.
- The often still very messy, disorganized, and non-compliant legal office environment is in real need of some organizing and simplifying principles – critically, efficiency is often seriously impaired by the time it takes to find documents and information.
- An ability to gauge adherence to agreed procedures immediately and visually can be powerful in organizations where there is a paucity of management information and metrics.

The basic principles of 5S were developed in Japan by Ohno (who developed Toyota's production system) and Shingo.[1] In Japanese businesses, 5S is commonly used at the outset of the organization's journey along process improvement, with the focus on changing mindset and housekeeping the physical environment.

Process principles of 5S

The eponymous five "s" words were originally Japanese (see brackets in the following bullet points), but have been translated into approximations in English that are now commonly used to designate the five component principles:

- Sort (*seiri*);
- Simplify or set in order (*seiton*);
- Sweep or shine (*seiso*);
- Standardize (*seiketsu*); and
- Sustain (*shitsuke*).

There are specific case studies for financial services businesses, retail, hotels, hospitals, and IT services. In many organizations, the focus has been on reorganizing and streamlining paper files and documents – with an obvious potential benefit for legal offices. Debashis Sarkar[2] has written a blueprint for 5S, based on the author's experience in catalyzing an enterprise-wide 5S implementation in India's largest private sector bank.

The introduction of 5S in service organizations can initiate the process improvement journey and begin to build a "quality culture" as it can in other industries.

Implementing 5S

Sort

Purpose – To remove from the workplace all items that are not required for current, ongoing work. Apply the principle: "If in doubt, move it out."

The list of items to be given a red tag and removed from the working floor to a holding area until either disposed of or stored elsewhere (after one week ideally) includes:

- Unneeded and unused files (includes closed files and those that could be stored in archive or cheaper storage not taking up working floor space);
- Old, defective, or broken supplies, equipment, files; and
- Junk mail, old memos/posters/ magazines.

In legal working environments the sheer build-up of files and documents, many of which should be held in less expensive and less accessible areas, can be a major issue. Combined with this, there is a significant challenge to law firms in particular who have to demonstrate how they are protecting client data in physical environments as well as electronic. Taking a strong 5S approach supports tackling these challenges.

Simplify

Purpose – To arrange all the remaining items in line with the workflow and in order to make them easy to locate and use.

Produce a current state map of the working floor and then redesign to create a future state map. The primary principles of the future state redesign are based around motion economy – keep everything if possible within arm's reach, organized in sequence. Obviously, with the increasing encroachment of electronic document management and storage, consideration has to be given as much to the accessibility of computer equipment, print/ copy, and telephony.

Sweep

Purpose – To organize a program of work that ensures the working floors remain clean and clear of excess materials.

In a manufacturing environment and any industry where health and safety is a dominant factor in working conditions, this component is fundamental, of course. In a legal office, this component is equally important. But the likely crucial issue is going to be assigning responsibility (and some authority) to individuals for continuous maintenance of file and paper archiving and destruction routines (this means daily and weekly, not quarterly or annually). In addition, those firms who have attempted to introduce some form of clear desk policy will know how difficult it is to retain the initial benefits without a rigorous approach to maintenance and policing.

Periodic inspections will be required, as will some interface with the objective setting and performance management process of the firm. Lawyers, in my experience, have tended to use big, almost "once in a lifetime" opportunities – in particular big building moves – to stimulate file and paper reduction exercises. This use of 5S, however, is about constant activity as part of the business of the firm.

Standardize

Purpose – To institute regular, sustainable routines that embed 5S practice in the working life of the business.

The activities established in sort, simplify, and sweep have to become regular, reflex parts of the activity of the organization. The standardize component of 5S is about setting this up.

At this stage, legal and other service organizations need to take care that they do institute techniques for ensuring the good practices introduced through 5S are not quickly forgotten – an experience project managers and management in legal businesses will be all too familiar with. But they must also be wary of standardizing and institutionalizing routines that drive out the autonomy of people to make any decisions about their workplace.

I have been engaged in projects that apply new, activity-based, or open plan ways of working to lawyers that are sometimes guilty of this excessive zeal to specify every detail of how people live their working lives. The procedures introduced should not be intrusive and should always be clearly justified by business need or benefit, not just by a desire to check the boxes.

Areas of particular importance include:

- Ensuring routines are not just established at an infrequent interval ("we had better check every so often" mentality, when it is inevitably too late to prevent serious damage to the initial successes) but sometimes weekly or even daily.
- 5S agreements which clarify what responsibilities individuals and teams (from the managing partner, CEO, or GC through the organization) have in respect of 5S and what the new procedures, processes, and measurements are.
- Visual process controls – Methods for rapidly assessing adherence to the 5S program. The aim of a well implemented program is to allow success and adherence to be immediately obvious "at a glance" and by anyone – a new visitor as well as a longstanding manager.

Sustain

Purpose – To introduce measurement and disciplines that ensure the standardized new processes continue to operate throughout the organization.

By using reporting mechanisms and periodic audits against a standard checklist organizations can monitor how well 5S is being maintained. Local teams or areas should be auditing their areas using a simple checklist. Examples of checklist questions include:

- Is the desk clear?
- Is furniture/equipment layout as per plans?
- Have closed and completed files been removed from the area for archiving or destruction?
- Are stationery and consumable supplies up to minimum levels?

Management at all levels need to be fully engaged in this effort and can assist the program by regularly communicating progress and celebrating success. Standards established under "standardize" need to be regularly reviewed and updated – these should be subject to the same continuous improvement philosophy emphasized throughout this report.

This first appeared as Tool 10 in Bull, C., The Legal Process Improvement Toolkit, *Ark Group, 2012.*

About the author

Chris Bull is a founding executive director of professional services consultancy Kingsmead Square. His consulting career stretches back to the mid-90s, when his focus was large financial services change projects as part of Ernst & Young's market-leading consulting team. The last two and a half years have been spent advising a wide range of professional service firms, with an emphasis on the legal market, on operational change and business management.

Chris is a regular speaker and writer on all aspects of the management of professional firms. His speaking, writing, and advisory work draws on a long track record of senior roles in the sector. As well as spells with Price Waterhouse and Ernst & Young, Chris was a member of the leadership team of law firm Osborne Clarke as the firm expanded rapidly and built a strong market position amongst the best UK firms. His roles there included chief executive, chief operating officer, and finance director over a hugely enjoyable 12-year period. As chief operating officer for Europe and the Americas at professional services outsourcing firm Integreon, he led the development of a legal and business process outsourcing offering that created a legal market leader.

Kingsmead Square was founded in 2013 by Chris and former-Barclays executive Louise Fleming. The firm has rapidly built an impressive client base of some of the most innovative and fast-growing professional service firms and new entrants to the market, including a roster of the most high profile alternative business structures and a number of large law firms.

Chris lives on the slopes of the Mendip Hills in Somerset in the south west of England. He "enjoys" running there and wherever he finds himself on his constant travels, and spends most of his spare time chasing around after his two children.

References

1. "Pioneers of Lean – Ohno & Shingo: An interview with Norman Bodek", Strategos website, viewed February 2012, see: www.strategosinc.com/nbodek.htm.
2. Sarkar, D., *Lean for Service Organizations and Offices – A Holistic Approach for Operational Excellence*, ASQ Press, 2007.

PART THREE

Project management, Lean Six Sigma, and KM

DMAIC: The framework

By Catherine Alman MacDonagh, CEO and founder, Legal Lean Six Sigma Institute

LEAN SIGMA uses a disciplined problem solving approach known as DMAIC, which stands for define, measure, analyze, improve, and control. This acronym is practically a mantra for process improvement practitioners and provides the framework for a process improvement project. After a project is prioritized and resourced, a good process improvement methodology must be used to deliver results reliably and following the DMAIC project execution methodology significantly improves the probability of project success.

DMAIC provides us with a proscribed sequence of steps that includes helpful ways of thinking through and analyzing many business questions and situations. We are encouraged to specifically define the problem or opportunity, gather data, analyze it, and only then to consider solutions. A more typical approach seems to be that we leap from having a fairly general notion of a situation to selecting a solution (and getting a bit stubborn about it) very quickly. As most people realize, this approach involves a great deal of guesswork. While it is inexpensive to guess, it can be very expensive (and a colossal waste of time) to guess wrong.

The five steps of DMAIC

The five DMAIC steps of define, measure, analyze, improve, and control are always performed in that exact sequence, without ever skipping steps.

1. **Define** the problem and why it needs to be solved – Here is where we carefully work through all the elements of a project charter;
2. **Measure** the current performance of the process – We measure the process in two dimensions: the performance level, or how well the process meets client expectations (process performance), and the resource requirements, or the time, people, equipment, etc., needed to carry out the process (process efficiency);
3. **Analyze** the opportunities to reduce waste or variation, identifying root causes;
4. **Improve** the process by developing solutions and identifying, implementing, and validating process changes; and
5. **Control** the process by implementing methods to ensure improvements will be sustainable and that the improvements are translated into benefits.

DMAIC also includes change management, communication, and avoidance of failure through the effective use of safeguards that are built into the framework. These safeguards include the all-important meetings with a steering committee, which follow the conclusion of each phase. This ensures that we are communicating as we progress with our projects and that we are employing good change management techniques.

Thus, after (and sometimes during) each phase, the process improvement project team meets with the project sponsor and a steering committee that is typically comprised of cross-functional leaders in the firm to pass through "gate reviews" or "toll gates". In these meetings, the steering committee holds the team responsible for completing specific deliverables that are required in each phase and ensures the team has addressed all the important considerations. They also offer additional perspective, information, suggestions, and feedback.

Thus, rather than complete a project from start to finish and then deliver the results, the approach demanded by process improvement is for our cross-functional and diverse team to regularly check-in with their project sponsor and engage in gate reviews with a group of decision makers that stays with the project from start to finish. This format builds in regular and ongoing communication for the duration of the project and provides a forum for the team to share their work as it progresses from diagnosing, measuring, and analyzing the process to finally developing improvement ideas. The shareholders also have opportunities to contribute their diverse perspectives, expertise, and resources on an ongoing basis – this is built in to the process of process improvement.

DMAIC builds in failure avoidance due to its design and rigor. It incorporates change management principles to ensure consensus is built as the project team progresses through each phase. Thus, there are numerous benefits to following the framework and to never skipping steps.

Step 1: Define

In the "define" phase, we will identify a serious business issue, one that is worthy of allocating resources to address. We initiate the project and carefully select and form the team. In the define phase, the project team will create and approve a project charter, working through each element, including the project plan. There have been occasions where teams working on a project have been unable to convince themselves that the project they have been asked to deliver is addressing something important enough to prioritize and resource. When that happens, realizing this fact early saves the firm more than time and resources – it prevents a firm from having a poor outcome or experience as the result of the process improvement efforts.

Because it is so important, Lean Sigma Principle 1, "specify value in the eyes of the client", is addressed at the very beginning of the project. In order to do so, we must also identify client requirements with tools such as "voice of the client", "moments of truth", "critical to quality", and a "client requirements summary". Finally, we will document the process using an "IPO (input, process, output) Diagram" (some organizations use SIPOC, which stands for suppliers, inputs, process, outputs, customer).

In addition to making sure that the project addresses an important client or business need, we employ good project management skills from the outset, making sure that the project scope and expectations are clear, that there is strong sponsorship and ownership, and that the problem (and the impact of the solution) can be measured and quantified. The team also begins to determine the most useful problem-solving approaches for the problem.

Step 2: Measure

In "measure" phase, we concentrate on Lean Sigma Principle 2: "Identify waste and variation by mapping and measuring the process". Thus, one of our first tasks is to map the process, using one or more of a variety of process map types. In this way, we gain a thorough understanding of the current state of our process (how we do things now); therefore, the team must have the ability to do both basic process mapping (IPO, block, top-down, detailed) and specialized mapping (swim lane map, spaghetti diagram, information flow diagram, time-value analysis), each of which shows the same process from a different vantage point.

A block diagram, for example, shows the whole process in just a few, key steps, while a top-down map shows sub-tasks under the main blocks. A detailed map shows all the steps with their relationships to all the other steps, including those that are wasteful, such as waiting and re-work. Specialized process maps are created to highlight particular kinds of issues or waste, such as handoffs, which are good places to start, since waste always accrues at boundaries. The goal is to capture the steps and thought processes, especially reviews and decision points, in a process.

Obviously, process maps are excellent tools for communications with clients and teams. They also allow for expedient onboarding of any new members and supports business development efforts by engaging prospective clients, referral sources, and strategic partners in conversations that elicit points of collaboration and differentiation. Typically, as soon as a process map is developed, teams immediately identify specific areas for improvement.

In the measure phase, the team also establishes a baseline of performance against which to measure progress, and measures many things in and about the process to identify waste and variation, defects, and causes of defects.

Then, we develop a measurement strategy and plan, using tools such as an issue diagram and/or measurement assessment tree. These tools allow the team to discuss what we want to measure in a structured format. Then, we attempt to gather information related to what we are interested in learning. We sometimes describe this gathering step as a big "fishing expedition" to see what can be learned and what is available. It is an iterative process to gather data, since a team might be (and often is) surprised by what is and what is not currently available in a firm either in terms of ease of access, quantity, or quality.

There is a hierarchy of data with respect to its usefulness and validity:

1. Reliable data that can be extracted from a system in electronic format;
2. Data that exists, but not in a convenient format (for example, paper files), which requires the team to figure out where it is, extract it, and then put it in a useful format, such as a spreadsheet;
3. Data that does not yet exist, but can be created using observation worksheets, surveys, and log sheets;
4. Externally available data, which usually is not specific to the firm, but may still be useful;
5. Estimations and opinion, which is better than nothing but not ideal. Usually, this involves asking several knowledgeable people and collating opinions; and, finally,
6. Anecdotes, which might be useful as a last resort. However, we have to be sure to understand the frequency of any occurrence rather than relying on one person's perception or experience.[1]

While the deep analysis of your data will take place in the next phase ("analyze"), long before that the team will need to understand what the data means and whether it has answered the questions raised so far in the project. Creating a visual representation of data is a powerful first step toward understanding, so each different data point that is collected is turned into charts and graphs (like Pareto charts, run charts, and histograms) to help the team consider all the information. Graphical data analysis is the process of making sense of the data, determining if it is adequate, and representing it in a way that informs and highlights key information. Thus, all the data that is gathered allows the team to begin describing the current state of the process very clearly and accurately; this is usually the first time a firm has ever truly understood how a process has been performing. Typically, it is very eye opening.

At this point in the project, a team will have a lot of data about the process, including process maps showing steps and waste, characterization data showing overall process capability and efficiency along several dimensions, and stratification data showing patterns and providing clues to causes. At this point, the team is ready to summarize and prioritize our areas of opportunity into a limited number of "focus areas" the team has become most interested in analyzing in greater detail in the next phase.

Finally, we use our graphical displays to help us create a storyboard that explains our logic to the steering committee. Now, the team is ready for another gate review. At this point in the project, the walls of the room in which the team is working are becoming increasingly covered with graphics, flip chart papers, and sticky notes. As such, it is ideal if the steering committee is able to be on site for this gate review.

Step 3: Analyze

In "analyze", we examine each focus area to identify and verify waste, defects, and determine root causes. Root cause analysis takes place in three steps:

1. Exploring;
2. Generating hypotheses; and
3. Verifying causes.

We use the data gathered in the measure phase to find patterns, trends, and other differences that suggest or support theories about the causes of waste or defects. We may need to gather further data to complete our analysis.

Our first step is to explore each focus area. We begin by assembling all the process maps and analyses that relate to each focus area. Using the Lean perspective, the team annotates each process map with notes highlighting non-value-added steps, waste, potential causes of problems, and ideas for further exploration. All process maps are useful for asking whether steps are non-value-added. In particular, the team looks for disconnects, decision points, inspection points, redundancies, and rework loops – and begins to illustrate why process maps can be such terrific tools to use in conversations with clients, prospective clients, and referral sources.

The team takes a similar approach to the graphical analyses, annotating each graph with notes about interesting observations, patterns, and trends. Finally, the team determines whether other tools or analyses might be useful in exploring the focus areas, and, for each focus area, creates a summary of interesting observations and questions created in this "explore" step.

The second step is to generate hypotheses for the causes of the waste or defects. At the end of the explore step, the team has a list of interesting observations, waste, problems, and questions. To find the root cause for defects, we use tools such as

"5 Whys" and/or cause and effect diagrams (also known as fishbone diagrams).

Lastly, the team uses data to verify or discard its hypotheses about causes. The team is then ready for its next gate review, having examined Focus Areas for bottlenecks, disconnects, and redundancies that might contribute to waste, analyzed data to understand potential root causes of problems and defects, developed root cause hypotheses for problems, and then investigated and verified root cause hypotheses to isolate "vital few" root causes.

Finally, the team gets to improve the process. At this point, it is (hopefully) clear how important it is to never skip steps in the DMAIC approach. If we were to begin to develop solutions too early, we most certainly would not identify the best solutions that are most able to provide us with the greatest improvement opportunities.

Step 4: Improve

In the "improve" phase, the team generates and develops creative solutions that address the root causes confirmed in the analyze phase. Tools such as problem statements, solutions filter, structured brainstorming techniques, and tree diagrams are used at this point.

Then, the team analyzes options and selects the best one, using a force field analysis, pros and cons analysis, weighted decision matrix, or an impact/ease matrix. After planning and executing a pilot test, the team conducts an after-action review. After an interim review with the steering committee and making refinements based on a pilot test, the firm is ready to implement full-scale improvements with detailed action planning, communication, training, troubleshooting, and ongoing measurement and performance measurement.

Step 5: Control

In the "control" phase, the process improvement project team develops approaches to maintain a process with an operation that is stable, predictable, and meets client requirements. This involves documenting the new process using tools such as standard operating procedures or statements of work, which describe how each step in the process will be performed, ideally in a standardized way.

All key project materials and artifacts should be preserved in a project repository, which ensures appropriate and ongoing availability of information about what has been done and what results were achieved by the project. Processes will always relate to, or overlap with, others in the firm, so those involved in other, future projects will undoubtedly find the team's work of interest. A project repository will explain the thought process behind your process improvements, and should follow the DMAIC flow of your project so that it can serve as a knowledge resource for the firm.

The team must complete the project by designing the controls, and defining metrics, responsibilities, and corrective actions. The project is finished when the firm has instituted process ownership to ensure that the benefits of the work are captured and the overall performance of the process is being monitored. The process owner has ultimate responsibility for maintaining the improvements achieved and educates others about the reasons for maintaining the improvements and the benefits derived from these. This person manages control and knows whether a process is performing adequately; if it is not, he or she is responsible for planning improvements.

Finally, the team compiles results data, confirming the achievement of the project charter goal. It will be important to report accomplishments, to open issues to senior management – and to celebrate success!

The Kaizen approach

In addition to DMAIC for full-scale projects, law firms I work with are seeing good results with the Kaizen approach. In the Lean Sigma world, Kaizen has come to mean a focused, fast, structured process improvement methodology. We think of a Kaizen as an accelerated problem-solving methodology, useful for problems of limited scope. We still go through the normal DMAIC sequence, but do so in a condensed time period, which makes it an ideal approach for firms with busy people on teams who do not typically all work in the same office.

One team member involved in a Kaizen project reported that "overall, the process worked well. I liked the Kaizen approach. The time frame/commitment worked well for me. After hearing tales of the prior (full scale DMAIC) projects and time involved in those I was very pleased to be involved with a Kaizen approach."

The way we structure our Kaizens is to begin with a call to prepare for our first team gathering, and then having a kick-off meeting, when we will carry out the "define" stage and plan the "measure" stage. The team then spends about a month collecting data and then comes back together for a three-day Kaizen workshop, where we will carry out as much of the remaining DMAIC sequence as we can, reviewing all the data and selecting focus areas on the first day (measure), then discussing causes and interrelationships (analyze) and developing solution alternatives and recommendations, plus implementing these as far as possible in the workshop (improve). The team continues to work on implementation and developing control schemes (improve and control phases) after the workshop, when working together effectively is less dependent on being in the same room at the same time.

In addition to providing us with a logical sequence of steps that have plenty of change management and communications built into the process, the DMAIC framework helps us to minimize or even eliminate typical project failures. It also helps us avoid the typical causes of poor achievement of promised results. To illustrate the point:

- Define helps us avoid picking the wrong problem to solve in the first place by having the team carefully define what it is they are trying to solve, determine the scope and so forth;
- The measure phase greatly improves our chances of selling our recommendations;
- Analyze safeguards against making poor recommendations; and
- The improve phase helps to ensure we develop the right solutions and avoid poor implementation.

Team members who started out as Six Sigma Yellow Belts and then earned their Green Belts after successfully completing their projects have this to say about the DMAIC framework:

- "Working as a team to improve a process allows you to collect a large amount of data, see different perspectives, and complete tasks more efficiently. DMAIC works."
- "Breaking down the project using the define, measure, analyze, improve, and control process really does work. It seems a bit overwhelming at first, but it gives a great result."

This first appeared as Chapter 3 in Alman MacDonagh, C., Lean Six Sigma for Law Firms, *Ark Group, 2014.*

About the author

Catherine Alman MacDonagh, JD is a Legal Lean Sigma Black Belt and a certified Six Sigma Green Belt. A former corporate counsel, Catherine is well known for her thought leadership and successes as a law firm executive. Now a highly rated speaker and consultant, she works with professional services firms to create competitive advantages and organizational transformation through the development, planning, and implementation of innovative strategies, process improvement projects, and business development training and coaching programs.

Catherine is an adjunct faculty at Suffolk Law School and at George Washington University (Master's in Law Firm Management). She is also the chief enthusiasm officer of The Legal Mocktail, an experiential networking training program, and has her own consulting practice, FIRM Guidance. She is a co-founder of the Legal Sales and Service Organization. In addition to *Lean Six Sigma for Law Firms,* Catherine is co-author of two books: *The Woman Lawyer's Rainmaking Game* and *The Law Firm Associate's Guide to Personal Marketing and Selling Skills.*

Please contact Catherine at Catherine@LegalLeanSigma.com, (+001) 857 272 5695, and on Twitter @cathmacdonagh.

References

1. "Outlining the problem of long delays, CIO Kevin Divine of the Hunoval Law Firm asked supervisors and staff in the firm's North Carolina default department how long they thought it took from file intake to sending out a notice of hearing to launch the foreclosure process. Anecdotally, they saw it as 14 to 20 days. But the crunched numbers tallied 69." See Carter, T., "Foreclosure firm goes statistical to improve speed and quality", *American Bar Association Journal* online; www.abajournal.com/magazine/article/foreclosure_firm_goes_statistical_to_improve_speed_and_quality.

Creating valuable knowledge in the firm through legal project management

By Lann Wasson, senior manager of knowledge management, Husch Blackwell LLP

In this expert analysis Lann Wasson, senior manager of knowledge management at Husch Blackwell LLP and a certified project management professional, discusses how effective legal project management can provide a wealth of knowledge to the firm's competitive advantage.

PRIOR TO the 2008 global financial crisis, market demand for legal services was so high that law firms rarely emphasized project management or efficiency as the hallmark of their offering. In the years that followed, however, corporate counsels' dissatisfaction with the status quo's assumption of value prompted many firms to consider alternatives to their current approach to pricing, staffing, and managing client matters. While some point to the immediate need of their institutional clients to control costs as the impetus for the greater focus on predictability, transparency, and efficiency, others contend that the onset of a buyer's market represents longer-term trends that were simply accelerated by the recession. Regardless of one's point of view, client demand for value has not lessened with the recovery and, to succeed in today's marketplace, firms need to demonstrate that their value proposition goes beyond their breadth and depth.

Since the launch of the ACC value challenge in 2008, many firms have gone to market with a branded form of legal project management (LPM), while others are still debating whether the investment in program development, training ,and organizational support can create lasting strategic value for their partnerships. Experimentation and piloting a range of approaches are still quite common as firms leverage existing internal resources in accounting, knowledge management, and information technology to estimate budgets, prepare alternative fee arrangements, identify precedents and workflows, and build out extranet solutions on a case by case basis. Whether the competency of project management becomes the norm depends on whether firms can use the knowledge gained in managing projects to create a sustainable competitive advantage.

What is often lost in these internal discussions is that while project management may address many of the pressing needs of clients, firms need a multidisciplinary approach – one that combines project management, KM, and process improvement to address both the short-term and long-term needs of clients. As some firms have already experienced during the re-negotiation of their alternative fees, clients want to lower the cost of legal services year after year and are intent on comparing the performance of their preferred vendors in order to work with firms which can continuously improve their efficiency. While a thorough discussion of all three areas is beyond the scope of this article, the benefits of a more coordinated effort are evident by looking at how project management can lay a foundation for process improvement activities and how a greater emphasis on process knowledge can also improve the utility and value of some of the basic techniques of project management.

For the purpose of this discussion, project management refers generally to the approach found in the Project Management Institute's (PMI) body of knowledge. As a more structured approach to service delivery, LPM addresses many of the immediate needs of clients by providing the tools and training to manage matters to a budget, demonstrate the business value of services delivered, and communicate changes to an engagement's scope, cost, or schedule. Unlike the way project management is used in industries such as construction and software development, LPM is often based on a simplified framework and toolset that allows lawyers, who are supervising matters, to continue to adapt to the unique characteristics and often adversarial dynamics of their work.

Launching the legal project management program

For those firms considering whether to launch a project management or process improvement initiative, the starting point for both is the basic project management toolset. When Husch Blackwell LLP began its first Lean Six Sigma project, the team spent some time reviewing the project management approaches from PMI ("Initiation", "Planning", "Execution", "Monitoring" and "Controlling", and "Closing"), Six Sigma ("Define", "Measure", "Analyze", "Improve" and "Control") and Lean ("Plan", "Do", "Check", "Act") to better understand both the fundamentals and the difference in emphasis in each method. Since project management is a tool-based approach, the team developed a matrix of tools and techniques from a variety of surveys and articles based on their frequency of use, use in service industries and use at the start of an initiative. Of the 50-odd tools compared in the matrix, the project charter, voice of the customer, brainstorming, waste, flow charting, root cause analysis and standard work ranked the highest according to our criteria. Although sometimes called by different names, many of these are the same tools and techniques used by project managers in their roles.

Launching an LPM program to address immediate client needs also creates a foundation for other improvement activities. Project management tools and techniques often start the process of standardizing work by creating checklists and templates, which can be reused on subsequent client projects. With a more structured approach to matter management in place at a practice level, lawyers acquire the habit of working off a framework, which allows them to adapt to improvements in design. From the tools and techniques, value stream maps can be built from flow charts of the current state, and checklists and templates can be incorporated into the appropriate phases, etc. Furthermore, since most law firms have not historically structured their billing data to capture cycle and lead times, project management can start the process of coding data which can be used down the road in value stream mapping.

Finally, law firms should consider beginning with a project management focus because there are likely to be greater internal resources in the firm's functional areas that can support this type of initiative. Often, certified project managers are working within a firm's project management office or are alongside other technical resources in the information technology or knowledge management organizations. Unless these resources are practice support lawyers, the challenge in many cases is that support personnel are often perceived solely as technical experts and may not have the understanding of legal processes nor the relationships with lawyers to communicate project management concepts and techniques in relevant ways without the use of technical jargon. Since project management is a mature discipline in other professional service industries, firms without internal human resources can usually identify consultants with both industry acumen, technical expertise and the required communication skills to assist with program development.

Creating knowledge that has competitive value

Without a strong emphasis on process knowledge, however, LPM can fall short of a program's original vision. As more lawyers begin practicing project management, what will distinguish law firms in the future is the process knowledge gained through dialogue in areas such as the triple constraint, the relationship between the logical design of templates and the drafting process, and lessons learned. Since dialogue takes time and requires teamwork both at a client team and practice level, law firms will likely need ongoing executive engagement to reinforce their importance. By looking at each of these three areas, one can see how a more coordinated approach – one that combines matter management with efficiency – can meet both the short term and long term needs of clients and create the edge firms are seeking in the marketplace.

One of project management's signature principles is the triple constraint, usually illustrated using a triangle that describes the interdependency between the scope, time and cost of a project. Changing one of the legs of the triangle, either by increasing or decreasing its value, will cause a change in not only one, but sometimes both, of the other constraints. In a law firm, the supervising lawyer is responsible for understanding how the project's sponsor prioritises these three areas and documenting the project's requirements, schedule, and budget. As a tactical approach to managing the work of a matter, changes are communicated as early as possible in order to make the best decisions on how to proceed and to minimize surprises that could damage the overall relationship.

From a process design perspective, however, the triple constraint ignores the underlying assumptions that cause this type of interdependency to occur. Since process improvement is focused on eliminating waste to increase both the velocity and quality in workflow, changing the design can in fact have a positive effect on all three at once. In addition to reducing wasted effort and time, process improvement methods also explicitly identify the specific instead of merely the type of knowledge resources and subject matter experts that can expedite certain tasks. By recognizing how a coordinated approach can mitigate or prevent the impact of the triple constraint in the status quo, project managers can document the instances where tradeoffs recur and discuss alternatives with knowledge management or process improvement personnel.

Another area of project management that requires more attention in a legal environment is the relationship between the logical design of documentation and the drafting process that creates it. In general, project management treats documents as artifacts that are managed either as inputs, outputs or deliverables to a phase of the project and is agnostic with regard to the efficiency of their design. Historically, the onus of selecting the optimal knowledge resource, template, or form has been left to the individual lawyer and their proficiency in using enterprise search tools, model document libraries, or their peer network. Even in practice groups, where the responsibility of managing model documents is delegated to a forms committee, the emphasis is usually on updating template language and reinforcing its consistent use, versus evaluating the drivers of drafting efficiency.

In a legal project where the primary deliverable could be a lengthy agreement, documents that are designed to reduce revision through standard formatting, by mapping information collected from the client or other parties during interviews or by staging language vetted by subject matter experts, can significantly improve quality and timeliness and reduce expense and client frustration. Supervising lawyers who are attuned to the design of documents can incorporate those elements into the project plan, and schedule and manage projects for greater efficiency. Only by engaging knowledge management and process improvement personnel, can project managers gain greater leverage from the artifacts they manage.

One of the most commonly discussed but least successfully applied techniques of project management is collecting and disseminating lessons learned. Many project management programmes assume that project knowledge should be captured during closure. In a legal setting, the activities during the closing phase of a matter often include the updating of project plans, templates, checklists, spreadsheets, and other tools to document both new tasks and assumptions, and to identify resources useful on subsequent matters. Sometimes, the supervising lawyer also obtains client feedback by listening to the sponsor in an interview or collecting survey data for comparison purposes.

Once these tasks are complete, the supervising lawyer then invites the primary stakeholders to a lessons learned session. During this meeting, the team reviews the primary objectives and results, and discusses their successes and mistakes and other exceptional circumstances. One of the team members usually records the salient points and provides a summary of the team's recommendations that are included in a searchable repository or through a corporate intranet or portal.

Anyone who has spent time in a more formal project setting in a law firm will tell you that it can be very challenging to complete the tasks of closure and hold a meaningful lessons learned session that contributes to the type of knowledge that is valuable to the rest of the practice. Generally, there are a number of reasons why these sessions fail. First and foremost is the pressure to complete other work in progress, since there are usually few internal incentives to spend more non-billable time after a matter has closed. Other obstacles include a lack of objectivity in meetings, the reluctance of associates and support staff to speak freely about mistakes and a lack of detail, because information decays over time unless it is recorded when incidents occur. Finally, since the focus is often on the particular matter and not the process as a whole, the emphasis of the discussion is more likely about the effectiveness of execution versus the quality of the design.

Although project management documents aspects of the process behind a matter during planning, it rarely evaluates the flow of information in ways that are common to process improvement methods. During a recent pilot in Husch Blackwell's mergers and acquisitions practice, a team of lawyers applied the tools and techniques of Lean Six Sigma to uncover the drivers of cost and quality in the transaction. Initially, it seemed that many of the techniques applied during a typical closing scenario would be equally useful during planning. However, as the team mapped out the process according to a standard set of variables and identified areas of wasted and repeated effort, it became clear that simply managing the existing flow was not sufficient. Only by changing some fundamental aspects of the transaction's design was the team able to reduce the overall anticipated cost and timeframe for the deal.

It is this kind of dialogue that is needed within project management programs to create the type of knowledge that has competitive value. Since effective project management relies heavily on historical information and experience, lessons learned should be captured throughout the life cycle of the project, as root cause analysis is applied. Embedding knowledge management within each phase of a project's life cycle also allows the supervising lawyer to monitor its progress at stage-gate reviews and make time for dialogue on the agenda. During closure, a final lessons learned session would then be able to extract the knowledge captured throughout the project and consider how these lessons can improve communication, collaboration, and other intellectual assets. Finally, developing forums internally to share knowledge gained on a variety of matters is a much more effective means of disseminating knowledge gained on projects than simply storing lessons learned documents in a database.

Project management is an essential first step towards meeting the pressing needs of clients for greater predictability, transparency, and efficiency, and can start the process of standardizing work in a law firm. Intellectual assets increase in value as lawyers' tacit experience is transformed into explicit resources and then used to refine another's tacit knowledge. Once this dynamic of the spiral of knowledge takes hold, it becomes extremely difficult for competitors to duplicate a practice group's efforts and present clients with more attractive alternatives.

For LPM to become a strategic asset, law firms must explicitly build in a greater emphasis on managing process knowledge than is typically found in many project management offerings. In conjunction with knowledge management and process improvement activities, project management can provide a wealth of knowledge from matters to improve a firm's leverage, but only if all three areas coordinate their efforts and communicate across silos. Firms investing in these initiatives should formally recognize knowledge management as one of the program objectives and create incentives to capture and share knowledge among client teams and practice areas.

This first appeared as Expert Analysis 7 in Ramasamy, S. (e.d.), Best Practices in Legal Knowledge Management, *Ark Group, 2011.*

About the author

Lann Wasson is senior manager of knowledge management at Husch Blackwell LLP and a certified project management professional. For the past 14 years he has worked with client teams and practice groups to support business and practice development through the use of technology systems and knowledge management strategies at the firm. Lann can be contacted at: lann.wasson@huschblackwell.com.

A simple legal project management framework

By Barbara J. Boake, partner, McCarthy Tétrault, and Rick A. Kathuria, national director, project management office and legal logistics, Gowlings

Legal mandates are projects

In order to enhance the chances of a successful outcome, legal mandates should be managed as projects. Lawyers who lead significant matters must accept the dual responsibility of:

- Performing the legal work; and
- Managing the project.

These are two distinct roles. Lawyers have historically been experts in performing only the first role. A legal project management framework provides a context within which lawyers can perform their less familiar role as project managers.

The framework divides a legal matter into its component project parts, which are distinct from its substantive legal or procedural parts. In this framework, these are referred to as project stages, project tasks, and project deliverables, in order to distinguish them from the substantive stages, tasks, and deliverables of a transaction or case.

Legal mandates have four project stages

Every legal matter can be broken down into four project stages:

- Define;
- Plan;
- Monitor; and
- Evaluate.

The project manager is responsible for moving the matter through each stage.

Figure 1 illustrates the four stages of a legal project life cycle. The five project management processes – Initiation, Planning, Execution, Monitoring, and Controlling and Closing – are depicted around the perimeter.

This legal project life cycle departs from strict project management theory in a number

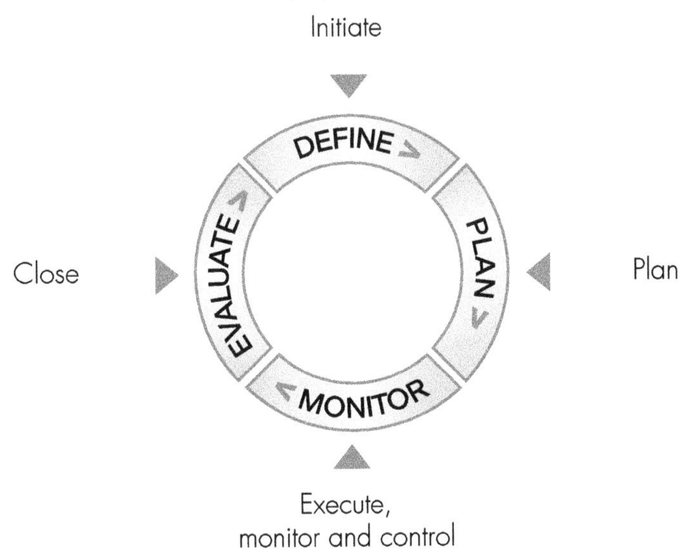

Figure 1: Legal project life cycle

of ways. The "execution" and "monitor/ control" processes have been combined into one project stage. Although these are quite separate functions that are often performed by different individuals, they co-exist over the same period in a legal matter. In addition, the execution of legal work is second nature to lawyers and not something that requires highlighting as a distinct stage in a legal project management model.

The project stages are named with a view to emphasizing those elements of project management about which lawyers, in particular, need reminding – "Define"; "Plan"; "Monitor"; and "Evaluate".

Each project stage has two project management tasks and one project management deliverable

In order to move a legal matter through each of the four stages, a project manager must ensure that the two tasks and one deliverable that are required at each stage are completed. These tasks and deliverables are depicted in Figure 2.

Your client participates at every stage of the project

One of the purposes of adopting a legal project management model is to provide law firms with the tools they need to give clients greater control over the cost and other outcomes of their legal matters. Consequently, before a project can move from one stage to the next, the client must agree with the project manager that the tasks and deliverables required at each preceding stage have been successfully completed. This requires continuous and effective communication between the project manager

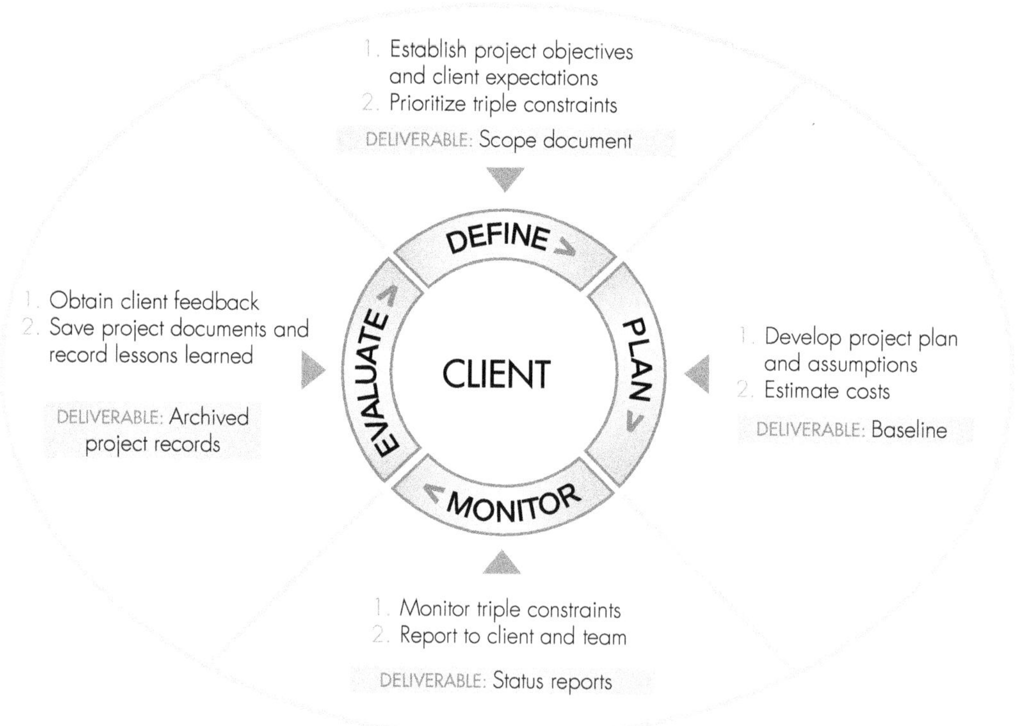

Figure 2: The legal project management framework

and client at every stage. Accordingly, the client is placed in the centre of the legal project management model as shown in Figure 2.

A project manager's responsibilities can be delegated

The lead lawyer on a matter will often delegate many of his/her responsibilities to another member of the team to perform or supervise the legal work. This is encouraged for project management responsibilities as well. However, given the importance of defining clear and achievable project objectives, it is recommended that the lead lawyer perform the tasks required in the first stage of a project. All other project management tasks and deliverables can be delegated to a more junior lawyer, a non-lawyer support individual or an administrative assistant, as appropriate.

Although delegation is encouraged, the lead lawyer must remain accountable to the client organization for the legal work product and to the sponsoring individual within that organization for the management of the project.

Designing a framework that works

Every law firm and legal department has its own unique culture and work style. The legal project management model described here was designed with the benefit of extensive trial and error, and uses tools and techniques that we believe are most relevant and useful in the practice of law. Although it should give you a head start, it will likely need to be refined or modified to work within your own organization.

Instituting project management in a law firm is not a quick fix. It is a challenge to the status quo that requires lawyers to change the way they have traditionally worked. Resistance is inevitable and the importance of strong and consistent leadership of the initiative should not be underestimated.

The business case for legal project management must be made and understood by the most senior levels of firm management before any work begins. As with any internal firm initiative, support from the firm leader will be critical to its success. The development of project management must be – and must be seen to be – one of your organization's highest priorities.

Careful consideration should be given to who will lead the initiative or, to use project management terminology, who will be the project "sponsor". This individual will set the objectives, timeline, and budget and will have important decisions to make at every stage of the process. Accordingly, they should have direct access to executive authority. The project sponsor should also be someone who is well versed in firm culture and in the organization's ability to embrace change.

You will need a project manager. Internal law firm projects involving significant non-billable commitments can be extremely difficult to manage and sustain. It will be important to choose a project manager who is able to set reasonable expectations and find ways to keep the project moving forward.

Finally, and most importantly, the project sponsor and project manager must firmly believe in the value of project management and be able to withstand the inevitable resistance they will encounter, so that the project can be kept on track.

This first appeared as Chapter 3 in Boake, B.J., and Kathuria, R.A., Project Management for Lawyers, *Ark Group, 2011.*

About the authors

Barbara J. Boake is a partner at McCarthy Tétrault in Toronto. She practices in the areas of bankruptcy, insolvency, and restructuring and advises clients in Canada, the US, and Europe. Barbara has extensive experience in acquisitions, dispositions, and restructurings of financially distressed corporations. Barbara has served on the firm's board of partners and its senior leadership team. She led the development and implementation of the firm's Dialogue Project Management® program.

In 2009, Barbara was named one of the Top 100 Most Powerful Women in Canada by the Women's Executive Network (WXN). She is listed in the 2013 edition of *Chambers Global: The World's Leading Lawyers for Business* as a leading lawyer in the area of restructuring and insolvency. In addition, she was named one of the top 40 international restructuring professionals under 40 by the *Global Insolvency and Restructuring Review*. In addition to her legal experience, Barbara has acted as a senior advisor to the Minister of Finance (Ontario). Barbara speaks regularly on all aspects of project management for the legal profession.

Rick A. Kathuria is a professional engineer (P.ENG), a certified management consultant (CMC), and a certified project management professional (PMP) with over 15 years of experience working on large international projects at top-tier consulting firms. He is the national director, project management office and legal logistics at Gowlings where he leads the firm's business transformation agenda and project management strategy (Gowlings Practical), applying process optimization and project management principles to the delivery of sophisticated legal services.

Prior to joining Gowlings, Rick led the project management initiative of another major Canadian law firm. In this capacity, he oversaw the introduction, development, and implementation of the firm's project management program.

Linking project management to pricing strategy

By Barbara J. Boake, partner, McCarthy Tétrault, and Rick A. Kathuria, national director, project management office and legal logistics, Gowlings

THE COMBINATION of significant increases in law firm costs and the downward pressure on hourly rates has forced law firms to re-examine their approach to managing profitability. In the current environment, law firms must focus much more carefully on pricing the work they do and look for ways to provide the same level of service to clients at a lower cost to the firm. They must also pay particular attention to profitability on a matter by matter basis, rather than simply multiplying rates by hours in an annual budgeting exercise.

In this chapter, we discuss how legal project management can contribute to matter profitability and help law firms manage some of the more common alternative fee arrangements (AFAs).

Basic practice economics

One of the benefits of a legal project management framework is that it encourages lawyers to be mindful of the factors that influence profitability when planning, pricing, and managing matters.

Figure 1 is a simple illustration of the positive and negative factors affecting law firm profitability.

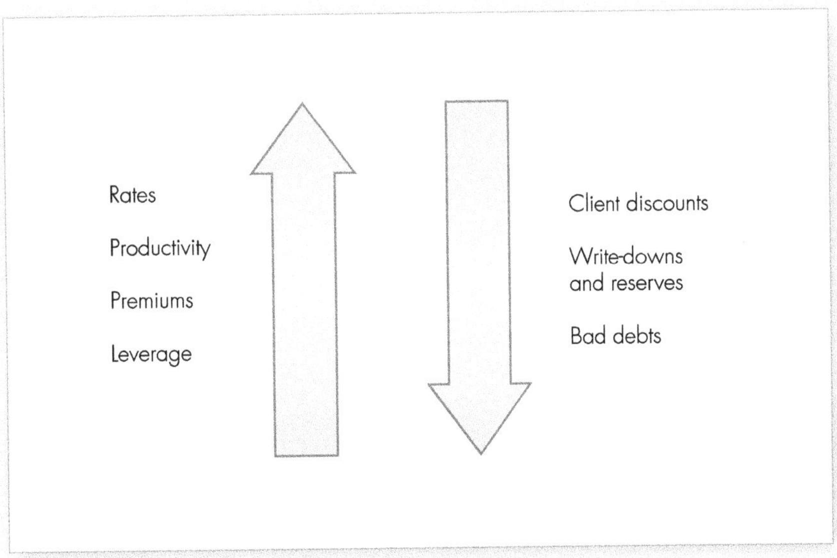

Figure 1: Variables that impact profitability

It is useful to look at the interplay between legal project management and some of the positive and negative profitability drivers in a law firm.

Leverage

Intelligent staffing will help to ensure that a matter is properly leveraged, allowing the firm to earn more profit per hour worked. Since equity partners share profits of the firm, their compensation is normally far greater than that of non-equity partners and associates, and the rate differential is typically not sufficient to compensate for this. Consequently, lawyers with the highest billable rates will typically be doing work at a higher cost to the firm.

Consider the comparative return on investment (ROI) for a senior partner and a junior associate, assuming both are producing the same number of billable hours per year, as illustrated in Table 1.

Rates

In a given year, lawyers will take on work of varying levels of difficulty and importance to clients, but will typically charge the same hourly rate on each engagement. This is a missed opportunity. It means that clients are paying too much for some matters and not enough for others. There are many instances where it may be appropriate to increase the set hourly rates of your leading experts to coincide with the importance and risk of a particular matter. By going through the discipline of properly defining the matter in the first stage of a project, you will discover whether cost is a relatively weak or relatively strong constraint and be in a position to set rates accordingly. In setting rates on a matter-by-matter basis, you may have an opportunity to increase matter profitability while at the same time meeting your clients' objectives.

Discounts

Since hourly billing is still the prevalent pricing model for legal services, law firms commonly respond to price pressure by offering discounted rates. This allows firms to continue to manage matters as hourly engagements, but it can materially reduce

	Partner	Junior associate
Compensation	$1,000,000	$150,000
Overhead	$300,000	$250,000
Total cost	$1,300,000	$400,000
Billable rate	$800/hr	$400/hr
Billable hours	1,800	1,800
Revenue	$1,440,000	$720,000
Net profit	$140,000	$320,000
ROI	11%	80%

Table 1: ROI comparison of a partner versus associate

profit margins. Premiums over hourly rates are rare and typically do not offset these discounts. Legal project management offers an alternative to discounts by providing clients with a structure for more reliable estimates and more predictable outcomes. Clients may be more comfortable accepting your firm's full hourly rates if they have some degree of certainty about the total number of hours required, and some measure of control over the management of the matter.

Write-downs and bad debts

If the proper change control process is followed for unexpected adjustments to scope, schedule, or cost, there should be no surprises when the final invoice is received, even if it is higher than originally agreed. The necessity for prompt and accurate time recording will ensure that interim invoices are complete and can be sent as soon as the work for the billing period is performed. In this way, a well-managed matter should reduce the likelihood of write-downs and bad debts.

Maximize profitability through efficiency and leverage

Law firm profits are typically measured in relation to an annual budget. Revenue is estimated using assumptions about rates, realization, and billable hours. Any budgeted increase in costs for the year is typically absorbed by corresponding rate increases. As long as clients are prepared to accept hourly billing and increased rates, there is no pressing need for law firms to reduce costs to maintain profitability. However, the market is challenging this business model and law firms must now find ways to improve efficiency and predictability in their matter management and pricing. There are a number of ways that a legal project management framework can help, and these are discussed further.

Use data from previous projects

There are many potential best practices for increasing efficiencies and reducing firm costs that can be identified if the projects have been properly evaluated.

Calculate averages

By analyzing historical information, you should be able to determine the average number of hours required to complete various types of work and make this a starting point in any future project plan. You should also be able to determine the range of seniority of professionals used on previous matters and identify the lowest-cost resource that is able to perform the required work. You can then develop standard staffing models for particular types of work that will produce an acceptable profit margin while delivering the quality that is expected by the client.

Choose resources wisely

There is obviously a wide variation in the amount of time it will take lawyers at different levels of seniority to complete the same task. Be mindful of the economics of this. Consider how staffing choices influence both the cost of the work to the firm and the price of the work to the client. Remember the differential ROI illustrated in Table 1 when allocating work between different levels of resources. Compare the amount of effort required by lawyers of differing levels of seniority, and determine which combinations are most advantageous from a profitability perspective. If the work satisfies the agreed level of quality and price, your client should be reasonably indifferent as to how the work gets done. For example, assume that a simple indemnification agreement is required as part of a larger transaction that is scheduled to close in two

	Partner	Junior associate
Hourly rate	$800/hr	$400/hr
Cost per hour (compensation + overhead)	$722/hr	$222/hr
Effort to perform work	2 hours	4 hours
Billing to client	$1,600	$1,600
Cost to the firm	$1,444	$888
Net profit	$156	$712

Table 2: The impact of leverage on matter profitability

days. The senior partner in charge of the transaction drafts the agreement, having concluded that the junior associate on the team would have taken twice as long to complete the task. Table 2 demonstrates the impact of this staffing choice.

In both cases, the client is billed $1,600 for the indemnification agreement. However, the net profit earned by the firm is materially different. Assigning the work to the junior associate would have resulted in a higher profit margin with no impact on the price of the work to the client. The senior partner who drafted the agreement herself because she was "too busy" to delegate the work, has cost the firm $556 in lost profits and missed the opportunity to spend two hours developing new business for the firm. The junior associate also missed the opportunity to improve his drafting skills.

Managing AFAs

As the market shifts further away from hourly billing in favor of fixed fees or strict budgets, law firms must learn how to provide an overall price that bears some relation to the value of the work to the client, while still making a profit on the matter. Law firms must also develop strategies to mitigate the risks that they are now being asked to bear in the event that fees exceed the agreed amount.

A legal project management framework can help in the ways discussed further.

Historical financial information

Historical financial information from previous engagements of the same type should be referred to as a matter of course before providing any fee arrangement where the firm is assuming a price risk. This should become a standard process for any firm considering AFAs. With sufficient historical data, your pricing conversations will be easier. You will be able to provide worst and best case scenarios on the length of time and range of fees for work that your firm engages in regularly. Eversheds believes that this is the most valuable result of legal project management.

Generating profit for the firm

When analyzing historical information, the key question is not whether the previous matters were performed within the agreed budget or fee cap, but whether matters that were performed according to plan generated a profit for the firm. Engagements that cannot generate an acceptable level of profit, even with the benefit of good project management, should be examined very carefully. Can they be priced or staffed differently to meet expected profit margins? If not, the firm should likely not accept work of this type in the future, unless there are other strategic reasons to do so.

Changes in the project plan

Where prior matters were profitable, consider what has changed since the matters were completed. Be sure to factor in any increases in rates and overhead, and any relevant changes in personnel.

Record assumptions

Record specific assumptions about tasks, times, and costs next to a description of the work to be undertaken. Include a list of these assumptions with any fixed price proposal or fee cap. These assumptions will enable you to clearly define the parameters of the price risk you have agreed to take on and will mitigate this risk.

Taking into account management time and experience when pricing

In determining the price of a fixed-fee engagement, do not overlook the time spent by the project manager and those to whom the project management responsibilities will be delegated. Once your lawyers become experienced project managers, these hours add value and are often properly chargeable. You may allocate the additional time among the various team members to whom the project management responsibilities have been assigned. Alternatively, an overall estimate of project management time could be calculated as a percentage of the final estimate and added to the price as a flat fee.

Justifying the price

If the objectives, constraints, and expectations have been properly defined, you will be in a much better position to determine and subsequently justify a proposed overall price for the work. You will know whether your client considers the matter business critical and you will know the relative priority of the scope, time, and cost constraints. If the matter is highly specialized, very time sensitive, or critical to the continuing financial strength of the business, it will obviously command a higher price.

Find other ways to add value

Focus on the project objectives that have been defined at the outset and determine if there are ways to add value to the project without adding additional costs. Would it assist your client in achieving their objectives if one of the team members (who might otherwise be under-utilized) were seconded to the client for the duration of the project? Could the firm conduct a legal education seminar on a topic of relevance to the project and invite the client's project team?

Cost variances

Cost variances will be a key concern for the firm and the reason for the variance must be determined promptly. Fixed-fee arrangements can be managed using a variety of monitoring processes. It is a good practice to increase the number of monitoring intervals for internal purposes and to consult the scope document, baseline, and the relevant assumptions at each interval to confirm that all work is in scope and that any out-of-scope work or changed assumptions are discussed immediately with the project sponsor.

This first appeared as Chapter 9 in Boake, B.J., and Kathuria, R.A., Project Management for Lawyers, *Ark Group, 2011.*

About the authors

Barbara J. Boake is a partner at McCarthy

Tétrault in Toronto. She practices in the areas of bankruptcy, insolvency, and restructuring and advises clients in Canada, the US, and Europe. Barbara has extensive experience in acquisitions, dispositions, and restructurings of financially distressed corporations. Barbara has served on the firm's board of partners and its senior leadership team. She led the development and implementation of the firm's Dialogue Project Management® program.

In 2009, Barbara was named one of the Top 100 Most Powerful Women in Canada by the Women's Executive Network (WXN). She is listed in the 2013 edition of *Chambers Global: The World's Leading Lawyers for Business* as a leading lawyer in the area of restructuring and insolvency. In addition, she was named one of the top 40 international restructuring professionals under 40 by the *Global Insolvency and Restructuring Review*. In addition to her legal experience, Barbara has acted as a senior advisor to the Minister of Finance (Ontario). Barbara speaks regularly on all aspects of project management for the legal profession.

Rick A. Kathuria is a professional engineer (P.ENG), a certified management consultant (CMC), and a certified project management professional (PMP) with over 15 years of experience working on large international projects at top-tier consulting firms. He is the national director, project management office and legal logistics at Gowlings where he leads the firm's business transformation agenda and project management strategy (Gowlings Practical), applying process optimization and project management principles to the delivery of sophisticated legal services.

Prior to joining Gowlings, Rick led the project management initiative of another major Canadian law firm. In this capacity, he oversaw the introduction, development, and implementation of the firm's project management program.

How KM staff can help drive successful legal project management initiatives

By Antony Smith, founder, Legal Project Management Limited

THE EMERGENCE of the discipline of legal project management (LPM) is relatively recent. I have heard it said that in terms of its overall maturity, LPM is now where KM was about ten years ago. Frankly, I am in no position to judge whether this is actually true but what I do know is that there are far fewer dedicated legal project managers in law firms compared to KM staff, and the adoption of software support tools for LPM is far lower than it is for KM.

Experienced KM staff should be in a good position to help with any LPM initiative in a law firm and they are often tasked in doing so. They understand what it takes for best practices to spread. They can also help directly with supplying best practice case plans, templates for all kinds of documents, and generally complimenting and enhancing the core skill-set of fee earners.

The aim of many LPM initiatives is that, ideally, fee earners apply project-based methods almost without thinking, simply as part of following the firm's standard way of working. As with any project, an LPM initiative needs to be planned, managed, and executed well if a firm is to reap maximum benefit from it. This can be something of a catch-22 for some firms as they do not have sufficient project management skills available to help improve the legal project management skills of their lawyers.

Knowledge management is itself quite a wide discipline and KM practitioners will often have diverse backgrounds. Some KM staff will feel very comfortable leading LPM implementation or improvement projects, and others will not. It is inconceivable, however, that a law firm will not seek to involve KM staff in some way when trying to develop its LPM capability.

So what factors should KM staff bear in mind when striving to make a success of an LPM initiative? Before I try to answer this question, I would like to remind you briefly what LPM is and why it is becoming increasingly important to law firms. I will then set out a project-based approach and provide some practical tips which should help make any LPM implementation project a successful one.

What is legal project management?

Legal project management by definition is the application of project management principles, methods, and techniques to the delivery of legal services. It can help lawyers better manage their individual matters and their practice as a whole.

This definition is deliberately broad. In operational terms LPM can cover a multitude of things, ranging from legal workflow process improvements to developing fee earner skill-sets (such as estimating and scoping matters).

Why do law firms want to develop their LPM capability?

The benefits of applying LPM are widely known. However, given that it is still relatively early in the overall development of LPM, realizing these benefits consistently remains challenging for law firms. Nevertheless, it is clear that LPM helps law firms to:

- Increase the predictability of fees, leading to increased confidence when devising pricing strategies;
- Estimate costs more accurately;
- Control costs more effectively;
- Identify and manage risks better;
- Become more agile when responding to client needs;
- Develop more streamlined legal delivery processes;
- Communicate more effectively with clients;
- Enjoy more productive relationships with clients;
- Improve realization rates;
- Increase profitability;
- Protect, and increase, business with current clients; and
- Acquire new clients.

In order to capture these benefits, law firms need to:

- Train fee earners and other related professionals about LPM principles and techniques;
- Create frameworks, processes, and procedures which support a project based approach to legal service delivery;
- Continue to develop the LPM skills (which is not the same as knowledge) of all relevant staff; and
- Embrace IT support systems (especially workflow and data analytics) whilst appreciating that successful implementation of LPM does not depend solely on IT.

How to start improving LPM capability

So, if your firm is about to begin an LPM initiative, either introducing LPM into the firm for the first time or seeking to improve existing LPM practices, what factors are likely to improve the likelihood of successful outcomes?

Think in terms of 'projects'

Leaving aside servicing "business-as-usual", at any one time there will be numerous projects going on in most law firms. Sometimes these projects are not even recognized as such. They may be referred to as "IT upgrades", "business improvement initiatives", or simply as "another round of marketing".

The fact is that any commercial endeavor can be classified, and therefore managed, as "a project". Blithely "doing stuff" which ties up resources without putting some project control around it is a recipe for disaster. So, the first thing to do is to recognize that tasks and activities which together make up an "LPM initiative" is "a project" in its own right. Hence someone needs to be in charge of the project and have accountability for deliverables.

Recognize that project management alone is not enough

Unfortunately, collecting and ordering tasks together as "a project" and putting some management control around it cannot guarantee successful outcomes. Even when organizations are enlightened enough to create "projects" and apply some form of project management to them, projects can often fail to deliver their hoped-for benefits.

What makes this situation rather depressing for professional project managers is that the main causes of project failure are well known, as are the key things to do to avoid such failure. There have been a number of studies which have investigated project failure and listed the most common reasons why projects fail. The list provided by the UK's (former) Office of Government Commerce (OGC) has been cited widely.[1] This list was first published in 2002, and it is still relevant today. According to the OGC at the time, projects fail because of:

1. A lack of clear links between the project and the organization's key strategic priorities, including agreed measures of success;
2. A lack of clear senior management [and Ministerial] ownership and leadership;
3. A lack of effective engagement with stakeholders;
4. A lack of skills and a proven approach to project management and risk management;
5. Too little attention to breaking development and implementation into manageable steps;
6. An evaluation of proposals driven by initial price rather than long-term value for money (especially securing delivery of business benefits);
7. A lack of understanding of, and contact with, the supply industry at senior levels in the organization; and
8. A lack of effective project team integration between clients, the supplier team, and the supply chain.

While this list comes with the caveat of being "aimed at those managing or otherwise involved in the delivery of projects across Government", it looks a pretty comprehensive list to me and, I'd argue, one that is also relevant to commercial organizations of all kinds, including law firms.

Aligning LPM with law firm strategy

I cannot imagine a law firm with a strategy which does not place clients, and the best means of servicing them, at its core. Legal project management is all about improving legal service delivery. Therefore, aligning any LPM initiative with a firm's strategy should be relatively straightforward.

Securing support of senior business owners and managers

In theory it should be equally straightforward to secure the support of senior business owners and managers. After all, an LPM initiative will (almost certainly) be aligned to the firm's strategy and all senior management staff buy into this, right?

Of course, and this is by no means confined to law firms, this is not always the case. In fact, it often falls upon the project team to secure full and enthusiastic support of senior stakeholders – something which some KM teams may be all too familiar with! Who might these senior stakeholders be and how can a project team make sure they are properly engaged with the project?

Project sponsor

In project management jargon, a project sponsor is the internal champion of a project. So, in a law firm, for any kind of LPM initiative it is almost certain that a senior partner will be the project's sponsor. The most important aspect of a project sponsor's role is to engage with other senior people within the firm (most obviously their fellow partners) and ensure that the project is fully resourced throughout. In effect, the project sponsor is the project champion.

Now, if the project sponsor is genuinely committed to LPM and has volunteered, perhaps even pushed for, the role of sponsor, then obviously the main issue for the project team is to retain their backing rather than securing it in the first place.

If the project sponsor has been asked to sponsor the LPM initiative by other partners they may be fairly lukewarm about LPM. This can be an awkward, but not impossible, situation. Perhaps the best advice here is to keep reminding the project sponsor of the benefits that LPM can bring to the firm and their practice area. Indeed, it may be best to focus on their practice area when considering any potential LPM pilot project. If you can ensure the project sponsor can see some early benefits from LPM, then they are much more likely to become fully engaged in the project and a more vocal advocate of LPM in the firm.

Other senior managers

LPM initiatives will often cut across departmental boundaries. People with roles in fee earning, business development, operational support (including IT and Finance), and of course KM, all have a legitimate interest in LPM initiatives. As a result, managing, or being part of, an "LPM initiative team" can be quite challenging. So how can this challenge be met and overcome?

I would suggest, and this will probably come as little surprise to experienced KM professionals, that particular emphasis should be placed on effective communications with team members, right from the start. Communications which are regular, clear, and concise not only advance the project, but also help promote a culture of transparency and collaboration amongst the team.

Communication effectiveness (or lack thereof) can make or break projects. It is estimated that professional project managers spend between 70 and 90 percent of their time on communications. Indeed, communication effectiveness is the key differentiator between the very best project managers and the rest.

Break projects down

A standard approach is to break projects down into a number of stages. It is quite common to see five distinct stages referred to: Initiation, Planning, Execution, Delivery, and Close. A project manager is responsible for steering a project through each of these stages.

From a project manager's perspective, most effort is (or should be) expended during the first two stages. It is during these stages that the scope of the project is defined, resources gathered, and a timetable agreed with the project sponsor and other key stakeholders (i.e. those who are affected by, or have a material interest in, the project).

Project initiation

The aim of the project initiation stage should be the agreement and signing-off, of a project initiation document (PID). This document captures the essential features of a project with reference to items such as project aim, scope, approach (i.e. how the work is to be performed), resources, budget, key risks, proposed schedule, and outline communications plan. Most importantly, a PID will state the acceptance criteria for project completion.

Project planning

During the planning stage, more detail is added to the outline plan and timetable encapsulated in the PID. Perhaps the best advice which can be given here is to go through the PID and ask repeatedly "what if" (for example: What if you do not get access to all resources? What if the timeline begins to slip?) and plan alternative scenarios based on your answers.

I would also suggest you talk, and walk plans through, with trusted colleagues. They may be able to spot things you have missed and perhaps offer reassurance that you really have asked enough "what-ifs"!

Project execution

During the project execution phase, project managers will be monitoring and controlling project progress. They will, if they have sufficient authority to do so, make changes to the project to keep it moving forward. They will also communicate this progress to all stakeholders regularly and escalate issues which are beyond their authority to the project sponsor.

During the execution stage a project manager needs to keep on top of all project issues and monitor risks (logs are set up for these). Another vital aspect of a project manager's role is managing scope creep. A project which changes during its lifetime is not necessarily a bad thing; indeed, it is to be expected. However, any changes in scope need to be agreed clearly with the project sponsor and other key stakeholders.

Project delivery

If the planning has been thorough enough and execution diligent, project delivery should be relatively straightforward. Projects will usually be made up of several delivery stages and indeed different types of deliverables. For example, LPM initiatives are likely to involve some legal process re-design and fee earner training (both areas in which KM teams are likely to be involved on some level), and IT support.

Project close

Project close is made up of several elements: the project sponsor signing off acceptance, the project team reviewing the project, and archiving useful project artefacts for potential re-use on other projects.

Some tactical ideas for LPM implementation

The above is a skeletal outline of a formal project management approach, but what tactical steps can KM teams take to help improve the chances of a successful LPM implementation project? The following is a list of suggestions:

- Start small with some pilot projects;
- Pilot with teams based in discrete practice areas and, ideally, pilot with those who are most interested in LPM (such people do exist – you just need to identify them in your firm);
- Encourage those who have experienced the benefits of LPM in pilot projects to spread the word to other areas of the practice;
- When designing LPM frameworks and practices it will probably help to think in terms of high level workflow. For any given practice area consider:
  - What activities are required to complete the most common matter types;
  - Who will (or who should) perform these activities;
  - What outputs are expected from these activities;
- Consider what kind of software support would help your LPM initiative. There are a number of software vendors which offer LPM support solutions. Alternatively, you may wish to investigate the feasibility of creating a software support tools in-house;
- Give serious consideration to branding your LPM initiative such that it becomes a recognizable aspect of the firm's practice; this helps make people in the firm feel as

though this version of LPM is theirs (which it is) and they will identify with it more readily; and

- Be prepared to engage outside experts who can offer LPM training, coaching, implementation, and consultancy advice. While it is essential that your firm "owns" its LPM implementation, objective advice from outside the firm can be invaluable.

This first appeared in Roche, H. (e.d.), Legal Knowledge Management: Insights and Practice, *Ark Group, 2013.*

About the author

Antony Smith is founder of Legal Project Management Limited and helps professionals in the legal sector to improve their project management capability. Antony does this by providing training, coaching, implementation, and consultancy services to legal service delivery organizations of all kinds.

Antony is a non-practicing solicitor with post-graduate level qualifications in law, computing, and project management. He is a member of the Association for Project Management (APM) and the Project Management Institute (PMI). He has spent his entire career in the legal services industry and has enjoyed project-based roles at Pinsent Masons, the School of Law Kings College London, Berrymans Lace Mawer, and Axxia/LexisNexis where he spent just over ten years in the role of strategic project manager

Reference

1. See: www.dfpni.gov.uk/content_-_successful_delivery-newpage-50.

Rethinking workflows: Re-engineering case management processes

By Scott Rechtschaffen, chief knowledge officer, Littler Mendelson

Over two years ago, Littler Mendelson set out to re-engineer the way that they handle the defense of administrative agency charges for their clients. Starting with a challenge posed by a major client and a desire to re-engineer the way their legal services could be delivered, they successfully developed and deployed Littler CaseSmart.

CaseSmart is an innovative case management process that has garnered new business for the firm, earned awards and accolades, and produced several lessons about the right way to implement change within a large law firm. In the following case study, Scott Rechtschaffen shares how Littler radically changed its case management processes.

Challenge and opportunity

In early 2010, with the ongoing recession and legal departments across the country looking for ways to reduce their costs, the general counsel at one of our major clients asked all of its outside counsel to propose ways to reduce its annual legal spend. Fortunately for Littler and, equally important, for the client, the shareholder responsible for managing the firm's work for the client saw this as an opportunity, not an obstacle.

At the time, Littler was handling about 25 percent of that client's administrative agency charges (i.e. charges filed with the federal Equal Employment Opportunity Commission or state agencies alleging, among other things, discrimination, harassment, or retaliation).

Recognizing that, for large employers, administrative agency charges have become commodity work – while some charges may have merit, many are the employment law equivalent of slip-and-fall nuisance filings – the shareholder wondered whether he could propose handling all of the client's administrative charges nationwide (over 1,000 charges annually) for a flat per-charge fee that would reduce the client's per-charge legal spend and its overall legal spend using multiple law firms, as it had been doing.

Reviewing the economics of the hundreds of charges our firm had handled for that client over the years and relying on the "law of large numbers", he calculated that a flat per-charge fee would enable the firm to balance those work-intensive cases (i.e. where the firm would lose money) against the charges that could be handled more expediently. However, handling this volume of charges profitably would require a much more efficient process than the firm had at the time.

The shareholder did not want to simply outsource portions of the work or to push the work down to the lowest-level associates; the firm's longstanding relationship with the client depended on ensuring the highest quality work product and results – even on commodity work.

The proposal would have to demonstrate that we had a plan to ensure the work product and results – as well as the client's relationship with the federal and state agencies – would not suffer.

The proposal would also have to demonstrate that this was not just a loss leader, an effort to get the client's higher value work; the shareholder knew that this client would see through and reject such an approach as not sustainable over the long run.

Creating a new approach

We quickly brought together a small team to assess the technology and alternative staffing solutions that would be needed to make the proposal viable. This initial working group consisted of attorneys intimately familiar with the client and several of the firm's C-level executives. We also brought in some outside technology consultants that were already working with the firm on other projects.

The CaseSmart approach developed by our team consisted of four main components:

1. A comprehensive process-flow analysis of administrative agency charge work;
2. A proprietary case management technology platform;
3. An alternative staffing model; and
4. Transparent access to all cases for the client.

1. Process-flow analysis

Our CaseSmart team brought together a number of the firm's subject matter experts experienced in handling administrative agency charges in a series of meetings.

Working with technologists and business analysts, we developed a step-by-step work-process map of how most attorneys manage the defense of administrative agency charges, from the moment the charge is received by the client to the point at which the matter is finally closed – whether by a settlement or a decision by the agency that is either favorable or adverse to the employer.

2. Proprietary platform

Based on the work-process analysis, and working with both in-house applications developers and outside consultants, we developed and deployed an advanced, proprietary case management platform designed to streamline and automate many of the steps required to process and manage charges.

A charge-intake process was developed to enable highly skilled administrators to enter into the system pertinent information that the attorneys handling the charges would need ready access to, such as:

1. Biographical data concerning the charge;
2. The alleged actors and the witnesses;
3. The pertinent facts and legal theories set forth in the charge; and
4. Personnel information pulled from the client's HR systems.

We then deployed document automation software to automate the production of standard, repetitive documents and also workflow tools to enable better case management and tracking of work product and deadlines.

We also developed a comprehensive Microsoft SharePoint TeamSite that would enable working attorneys to readily access client information, legal research, and template documents, and to communicate efficiently using social networking tools.

The overall platform was designed to enable attorneys to work more efficiently and to ensure overall quality and performance standards were maintained.

3. Alternative staffing model

Our team had analyzed the work processes,

identifying inefficiencies. We had looked for:

- Tasks being performed by shareholders that could be performed by associates;
- Tasks being performed by associates that administrative staff could perform; and
- Tasks administrative staff were performing that technology should be handling.

Based on this analysis, we recognized that the traditional shareholder-associate-secretary model of handling a matter would not enable the type of efficient task-based process we envisioned; we knew that CaseSmart would require an alternative staffing model.

The first step was to develop the highly skilled administrative staff that could perform the intake and initial discovery processes effectively and also oversee case management.

The next step was to recruit a cadre of flex-time attorneys (FTA) with substantial experience in handling administrative charges and who desired an alternative career path that included flexibility and greater control over their schedules and caseloads. We decided early on that these FTAs would be staff attorneys, not outsourced or contract attorneys.

One of our reasons for using FTAs, as opposed to traditional associates, was that FTAs could be deployed in a task-based, team structure; they would only work on CaseSmart charges and they would be dedicated to specific clients.

In this way, they would become extremely proficient at performing a specific set of tasks – investigating and defending administrative agency charges – and they would get to know their assigned client's culture, operational issues, and personnel extremely well, thus greatly increasing their efficiency.

A team of responsible supervising attorneys (RSA) – shareholders experienced in working with specific clients – would supervise the FTAs, assisting them in performing a risk analysis. This is a critical step in determining early on whether the charge should be settled or defended, based on parameters defined by the client in advance.

The RSAs would also be responsible for reviewing the FTAs' work product, particularly statements of position submitted to the agency in defense of the employer's position.

Finally, each client would be assigned an overall project director to oversee the work of the administrative team, the FTAs, and the RSAs, and to be the client's primary point of contact for overall case management issues.

4. Matter transparency

One of the keys to the CaseSmart system is that it is an outsourced model: the client effectively turns over management of individual charge matters to our firm, enabling the client to focus, instead, on how we are handling its overall caseload. This eliminates the inefficiencies that arise from back-and-forth decision-making on individual charges, enabling the client to deploy its internal legal team to handle higher-value matters.

But, to make this model work, the client has to have the management tools necessary to monitor how effectively the overall caseload is being handled. The client needs to feel confident that individual cases are not languishing, that the firm is not settling too many cases or spending too much on settlements, and that the quality of the work product meets the standards the client expects.

To enable the client to monitor these critical issues, the system was designed to provide transparent access through an online dashboard that enables the client to see the status of any given matter – the charge data, agency documents, and the attorney's work product – as well as to see the status of all of its matters at a macro level.

It enables clients to see real-time key performance indicators showing, amongst other things, the number of charges being settled versus the number of charges being defended, the average settlement amount, and the length of time it takes to resolve charges.

More importantly, the dashboard provides clients with actionable intelligence about what is going on within their own organizations. Clients can see the types of claims being filed and the location of these claims (such as regions or facilities that are encountering larger numbers of charges), enabling them to make informed operational decisions (such as which regions or facilities require additional management training or which internal policies might require review and revision).

Lessons learned

Our approach has proven successful on many levels. Over the past two years, we have managed more than 3,400 administrative agency charges through the system, exceeding expectations in terms of quality of work product and results, efficiency, cost savings to the clients, and realization for the firm.

Our firm has brought new clients onto the system and has garnered industry accolades and industry honors, including the International Legal Technology Association's 2011 project of the year award and the 2012 InnovAction award from the College of Law Practice Management.

While the accolades and the new business are, of course, tremendously rewarding, the success of the project has provided an opportunity to re-evaluate what really works in terms of legal process re-engineering and how law firms can adjust to the "new normal" for delivering legal services.

What follows are just a few of the lessons we learned from the CaseSmart project.

1. It really does take a village to implement meaningful change

While our initial team consisted of a small core group, the real operational team would eventually involve over 60 individuals across virtually every corporate department in the firm and five outside technology providers.

For example, initial operational plans were adjusted once our chief information security officer and his team got involved and focused on the need to ensure client data was effectively protected, particularly with FTAs working remotely. Specific security precautions were implemented to ensure data security at every step in the process.

Our chief product officer and his team helped to develop the processes followed by the administrative team to ensure the efficient processing of client information.

The professional development staff were instrumental in designing a program to ensure the FTAs were integrated into the firm's training and development programs.

Our finance and accounting department was critical in developing protocols to ensure there is meaningful case management reporting for both the firm's and the client's benefit.

2. Support from firm leadership is critical

From the very beginning, our management committee and senior leadership recognized the possibilities of the project and the potential future impact the project could have on the way we deliver legal services.

Indeed, our chief operating officer was a member of the CaseSmart leadership team from the outset and was involved in most of the major decision-making throughout the development phase.

3. Think big, start small

Any effort to entirely re-engineer the way a large well-established firm does business will encounter insurmountable obstacles. A better approach is to focus on a small area of the firm's practice, demonstrate success, and offer to replicate that success in other areas.

We were able to take one process (the management of administrative agency charges), improve it significantly, and show it as a successful model for other areas of practice. Other practice groups have since requested help with re-engineering the way that they deliver legal services.

We are now looking at applying our CaseSmart approach to single plaintiff litigation, wage-hour class actions, and other aspects of the labor and employment practice group.

4. The "new normal" poses challenges, but also opportunities

Many attorneys have confronted the dramatic changes in the legal industry by hoping that the good old days of ever-rising rates and limited client pushback will return.

The firms that will have the greatest success in the new paradigm, however, will realize that the good old days are not coming back and they must try equally dramatic approaches to re-thinking their business strategies. By doing so, they can find new ways of generating increased revenue, realization, and profitability, as well as delivering greater value to their clients.

Key takeaway points:

1. It really does take a village to implement meaningful change, so plan to include all relevant people early on;
2. Support from the firm's management committee and senior leadership is critical;
3. Think big, start small – Focus on a small area of a firm's practice, demonstrate success, and offer to replicate that success in other areas; and
4. The "new normal" poses challenges but also opportunities – Consider dramatic approaches when rethinking your business strategies.

A version of this article first appeared in Managing Partner *magazine in January 2013.*

About the author

As chief knowledge officer of Littler Mendelson P.C., Scott D. Rechtschaffen leads the firm's effort to provide innovative client services by integrating new technologies and work processes, and enabling attorneys and clients to access the collective knowledge and experience of the firm's more than 1,000 attorneys. He combines over 25 years of experience representing companies in every area of labor and employment law with a broad understanding of technology to help the firm's attorneys and their clients in tailoring unique solutions that enhance the firm's ability to deliver legal information and legal services to its clients.

Scott heads the firm's knowledge management (KM) department comprising dedicated, full-time knowledge management attorneys – who are all experienced employment and labor law attorneys, technologists, research specialists, and administrative support. The KM team supports the firm's attorneys, practice groups, and major firm initiatives. He has been a key member of the multi-disciplinary team that developed the award-winning Littler CaseSmart® approach to legal case management. He oversees KM's work on the firm's electronic and print publications – *The National Employer*, blogs and newsletter alerts, Smart Search – the firm's internal search engine, LittlerNet – the firm's intranet portal, Littler's Extranets, and online subscription services – Littler GPS® and Littler Monitor.

In addition, Scott is responsible for the firm's Executive Employer® Conference, an annual gathering of in-house counsel and human resources professionals representing some of the country's leading organizations. He was the co-creator of Winning Through Prevention: The Littler Employment Law Challenge, an innovative teaching tool designed to enhance the training of managers and supervisors. Scott has written extensively and has published articles in national publications on human resources management, knowledge management, and legal technology. He regularly speaks at knowledge management seminars and legal technology conferences organized by the American Bar Association's Law Practice Management Section, Association of Corporate Counsel, American Lawyer Media, Legal Marketing Association, International Legal Technology Association, ARK Group, and other professional organizations.

PART FOUR

Online delivery for process improvement and client satisfaction

Why deliver services online?

By Stephanie Kimbro, fellow, Stanford Law School Center on the Legal Profession and co-director, Center for Law Practice Technology

THIS QUESTION begins the important analysis that a law firm must go through before establishing a strategy for online legal service delivery. What are the primary reasons the law firm wants to deliver services online? The firm must determine those reasons to select the appropriate method and approach to developing a model of online delivery. Some of the reasons for choosing online delivery might include:

- Expanding the firm's reach into other territories and regions, including a desire to expand its client base;
- Creating a completely separate, new source of revenue for the law firm;
- Competing with other law firms and companies delivering online services;
- Building an online brand and marketing strategy to expand the firm's reputation as being innovative and forward-thinking;
- Using online services as an amenity to retain existing and recurring full service clients;
- Lowering overhead by taking certain law firm procedures and operations online, including the use of remote working arrangements for lawyers and support staff;
- Going paperless and transitioning the firm to a cloud-based technology for all its practice management and administrative operations;
- Creating better work/life balance and flexibility for firm members; and
- Unbundling and repackaging its legal service offerings to increase efficiency of operations to serve more clients and more efficiently serve its existing client base.

A law firm may find any one or a variety of these reasons for choosing to deliver legal services online. Depending on the motivating factors for adding online delivery, the firm's selection of the model of delivery, the technology platform and its features, the billing methods used, and other decisions for the development of online delivery will vary. For example, a firm whose motivating factor for adding online services is to transition the existing firm to a cloud-based model will be more focused on selecting a technology platform that will enable the conversion of the firm's existing data into the cloud. A firm that is focused on adding online services as an amenity to its existing law firm offerings for purposes of competition and marketing may select a different online service platform that builds into the firm's online brand building and marketing strategy. Lawyers who are interested in online delivery as a way to ease into retirement from a traditional law firm model may focus on a technology set-up that allows for more flexibility when transitioning from one model to another, rather than on a robust online practice management system with online delivery features. The process of researching and deciding which structure of online delivery would work best begins after the firm determines the motivating reasons for adding online delivery.

What is the competition?

In addition to regulatory changes in some countries which make it possible for unlicensed lawyers to deliver legal services online, the legal profession has seen increased competition in online delivery across the globe. For example, LegalZoom filed an S-1 form in the United States noting that it planned to raise $120 million in an initial public offering (IPO). In this filing, the company revealed that it had served almost two million customers in its ten years of operations. In one year alone, 2011, the company claimed to fill 490,000 orders for online legal services. For lawyers in the United States, these numbers are nothing to ignore. These are individuals who would have either turned to self-help solutions or retained the services of a lawyer.

LegalZoom has been joined by many new players that are grabbing the attention of online consumers seeking assistance. For lawyers internationally, it is worth taking a look at the non-lawyer owned companies, such as Rocket Lawyer, that might be providing legal services online and estimating the amount of business that is being taken from licensed lawyers through these alternative delivery channels. In some circumstances, it may be possible for law firms to collaborate with these branded networks delivering online services as part of a larger online marketing strategy.

There are other interesting developments occurring that may shape the competition for online legal services. Recently, SunTrust Bank, a major bank in the United States, partnered with Business Centric Services Group, Inc. on the development of a Business Hub to deliver legal and other services to small business banking clients. Both Epoq Legal, a company based in the UK, and DirectLaw, a US based company, are providing technology components to this project. MozyPro, PlanHQ, Moonfruit, and FreeAgent are also providing software that would be useful to small business clients of the banking giant. All of the tools provided in the Hub cost the user $25 a month, which may be debited from the user's SunTrust banking account. This type of holistic care and convenience for small business owners is something that a solo or small law firm would have trouble replicating.

In terms of competition from other lawyers adding online legal services, the adoption of this business model is still in the beginning stages. Lawyers opening law firms that provide online services in many jurisdictions may have first-mover advantage over the competition. Overall, the number of lawyers moving to cloud-based technology has increased. In the United States, the 2013 American Bar Association Legal Technology Survey Report stated that the percentage of lawyers who say they use cloud-based technology rose to 31 percent over the 21 percent seen in 2012.[1] However, their use of technology appears to be focused on systems for practice management rather than technology to deliver legal services online. The report also noted that only 5 percent of lawyers who took the survey stated that they had a "virtual law practice". The number reporting a virtual law practice in 2012 was 7 percent. In the United States, the term "virtual law practice" is used to describe a practice where the lawyer has no physical law office and delivers services to clients online. Even including the lawyers that did not claim to operate a virtual law practice in the States, 35 percent of lawyers responding to the survey said they offered unbundled legal services. The survey described these services as "specific, stand-alone services like document preparation, offered as an alternative to full representation". Accordingly, while we do not have similar statistics for other countries, we can most likely predict that lawyers across the globe will continue to increasingly adopt cloud-based technology solutions for their practices. These solutions will either come with tools for online delivery or facilitate the unbundling of services which may then be delivered online. Judging the competition for online services in terms of other lawyers and law firms may be a simple task at this point, but that will change as more firms see the benefits of delivering online.

Finding ways to differentiate a firm's online options from these competitors and setting up the value of the professional expertise is going to be an ongoing task for any firm considering delivering online legal services. However, without providing prospective clients with some form of online delivery that meets consumer demand for affordability and convenience, it will be difficult for law firms in the future to remain competitive, especially smaller firms and those that provide basic, personal, or consumer legal services.

What are the benefits for the public?

The public is accustomed to making purchases online and many of them conduct activities online through secure client portals, such as earning educational degrees, shopping, banking, investing, and paying taxes. Consumers are used to fixed fee prices for services and products sold online. Accordingly, when they need legal assistance, they expect to find online legal services that will provide them with the following information:

- Do I have a legal need?
- How much is it going to cost to resolve this legal issue?
- How long is the process going to take and what is that process?
- Prompt updates on their matter along with responses to emails, phone calls, and complaints they may have.

In addition to this, online clients expect that services will be delivered at a lower cost than traditional in-person legal services and that these services will be online and available 24/7 as opposed to traditional business hours. They also expect the firm to provide links to other resources and self-help legal services online so they may empower themselves to take action or become more educated about the process while working with the firm through the client portal.

These days the public has other options to obtain legal services online through branded networks and non-lawyer owner companies providing legal assistance. Law firms must distinguish themselves from these other options by emphasizing the value that a licensed lawyer adds to the delivery of online legal services. The primary benefit to the public of lawyers operating online legal services is that they are provided with an alternative, potentially higher quality option for legal assistance than a legal form or document that is sold to a consumer by an individual or entity without formal legal training and experience. Lawyers delivering legal services online increases access to justice internationally for a large number of middle-income individuals who need the affordability and convenience of online delivery, but the experience and expertise of a licensed legal professional. While the benefits of adding online services to a law firm are numerous, it is this potential to serve the public that should encourage more widespread adoption of online services by the profession.

What are the different structures of online delivery?

The key component to online delivery regardless of the chosen structure for integration is the use of a secure client portal. A secure client portal is a feature posted on a website where the user is provided with their own unique username and password. This information is used to log into a secure account page which is encrypted.

With online legal services for law firms, the client portal is posted on the law firm's website. When the client registers or logs in, they are redirected to a secure space that is hosted by the technology vendor that the law firm has chosen for the purposes of the platform for online delivery. If the firm has created its own custom client portal and account access platform, then it redirects the client out to this space. However, most law firms do not have the thousands of dollars it would take to create a customized account access system. Instead, most firms rely on a form of cloud computing called "software as a service" (SaaS) to provide the features of a secure client portal.

When a law firm uses a SaaS product to create an online delivery option, it is providing confidential law office data to a third party provider. (There are certain ethical issues that may be raised by this, which will not be entered into here.) With SaaS, the technology company that owns the platform provides the lawyer with a license to use the software. The software is hosted on servers which may or may not be owned by the company. Many cloud-based technology providers will actually lease server space from separate companies that own data centers. Data centers are multimillion dollar facilities that are often located in undisclosed locations for increased security. Tier 4 data centers are the most secure level of center and are what the law firm should look for when investigating the hosting capabilities of its SaaS provider. When the license is terminated for the service, the company removes the lawyer's data from the server. Many SaaS vendors will provide geo-redundancy of servers, which means that the data is backed up in data centers in two different locations.

After selecting a client portal technology or customizing its own system, a law firm must then decide how it intends to market or brand its online services depending on the strategy for structuring online delivery in the law firm, and for developing an online client base.

There are three primary structures of online delivery, detailed below.

A completely web-based delivery of online legal services

In this model, the lawyer or law firm does not operate a traditional bricks and mortar law office space, but works only with clients online. This model requires that the lawyer provide almost all unbundled legal services rather than full service representation. The lawyer may work from a home office or leased, temporary office space but does not necessarily disclose this location to their clients.

An additional online component

A traditional law firm may add an online component and use it as a marketing strategy as an amenity for existing, in-person, full service clients. The firm may also use it as a way to develop a completely online client base for unbundled services to generate additional client revenue.

A virtual law firm model

A law firm may create a virtual law firm model where both online and in-person services are provided but the lawyers work remotely from each other, communicating through technology to create a law firm culture and working with administrative and support staff online. Both home offices and leased office spaces may be used by lawyers in the firm when needed to meet with clients. This model allows a single law firm to have a broader geographical reach than a traditional law firm and potentially expand its client base across multiple cities and regions.

Who will be in charge?

The first step in the process for integrating online legal services in law practice is the establishment of a clear and achievable strategy for implementation. The law firm may wish to choose one individual who will be responsible for leading the implementation of online legal services, or form a committee that will set a clear and achievable strategy that could successfully be achieved by the firm's existing team of lawyers, staff, and support. The individual or committee spearheading these changes should have a solid knowledge of the internal processes and procedures of the law firm as well as having a solid grasp of the firm's existing technology resources. If the firm has an IT consultant with intimate knowledge of the firm's technology, they should be included in this decision-making process but should not be the sole individual guiding the process. They will need assistance from lawyers with experience in the practice areas that the firm will be unbundling to deliver online. The firm would also be advised to keep its members and support staff informed about the progress of these changes. In order for online legal services to be implemented in a law firm, especially with the integration of new law firm technology such as a client portal system, everyone in the firm will need some training and patience in adding this to their regular workday routine. Determining who in the firm will be in charge of spearheading the move to online legal services will greatly facilitate the transition for both the firm and its clients.

Case study: Samuel Phillips

Samuel Phillips is a law firm based in Newcastle upon Tyne serving clients in Tyneside, Wearside, Northumberland, Durham, and elsewhere in the UK through its online service delivery. The firm has a separate website delivering online employment law services and has created an iPhone app which provides information regarding employment law and compliance issues.

Consumers may select from a list of services offered for fixed fees online. After selecting the appropriate employment law document, the consumer purchases it directly online through a secure checkout, completes the questions asked in the document online, and submits it to the firm for review. The law firm reviews the document and it is uploaded to the client's secure client portal access to download and use.

In addition to online document purchase and submitting it for review, consumers may contact a lawyer of the firm at any time for consultation or to move from the online legal service delivery to full services.

Establishing a clear and achievable strategy for online delivery

The decision to deliver online legal services begins with an analysis of the existing law firm structure and services that are offered. There are different ways that online legal service delivery could be integrated into an existing law firm model, as already outlined above. So, how does a firm make the decision about which model of online delivery would be most effective for its clients and its existing business?

Begin with an internal analysis

In order for a law firm to begin the process of deciding what type of model for online delivery it needs and how to integrate online legal services, it must first take a step back and look at its existing practice areas and the services it currently provides to clients in a traditional manner. The firm should start with one practice area at a time and analyze the typical intake and management procedure for the case through to the termination of the relationship with a client. Noting which individuals at the firm are responsible at each step and stage in a case is also important as well as what technology, if any, is used at each stage.

The following list of questions may be a useful starting point:

1. What are the processes and procedures for the creation of new cases?
2. What is the client intake process and how is data collected from the client regarding the matter?
3. Who in the firm works with the client first and how is the matter processed through to associates and partners in the firm?
4. What technology platforms or systems are used with the matter? For example, does the firm rely on a document automation and assembly technology system or use a document management system to pull similar legal documents out for repurposing by the firm?
5. What is the process for meeting with the client? Is this done in the office, by phone, video conferencing, or through a combination of communication methods? With matters such as complex litigation, the task of breaking down the firm's process and procedures may take more time and may be more complicated.

After the firm has answered these questions and gone through this analysis, it will have a better handle on what type of technology, support staff, training, and additional administrative procedures will be needed to add online legal services to the firm's existing operations. The firm may wish to create a business plan that specifically lays out the firm's plans to integrate online services and scale them as that part of the practice develops. Business plans for online legal services should be fluid documents that will need to be analyzed and adjusted as the practice develops.

What are unbundled legal services?

Essentially, the above list of questions requires that a firm must "unbundle" its existing practice and then analyze what part of it, if any, might be delivered online. After unbundling its practice, it can then go back and "rebundle" it with the integrated online legal services. Some law firms may be unbundling their services for clients already without realizing they are doing so. Unbundled, or limited scope legal services is the practice of providing the client with only certain portions of their legal need while permitting them to complete the remainder of the task to solve their own legal need. An example would be assisting the client in creating a corporate document, but giving them instructions for full execution of that document and leaving it up to them to complete the matter. There are best practices for unbundling which must be followed.

Rebundling services with online delivery

After going through the above process, the firm should then analyze the findings by asking the following questions to assist it in rebundling some or all of its services:

1. What processes may be taken online for delivery through a secure client portal space?
2. What existing legal technology platforms or systems does your firm employ that it would need to keep in place or find a way to transfer over to a more robust online client management system? How easily can this data be transferred into a new system? What practice management tools and administrative tasks does the firm most need to have in any online delivery system?
3. Do you want to limit your online services to transactions-based work for online clients, such as limiting your online offerings to legal forms or document generation, or find a way to deliver services online that include guidance and consulting through video conference, real-time chat, and other methods of communication with clients and colleagues online?
4. What would be the acceptance rate by the other members of the firm and support staff if the firm implements these changes? What kinds of training and support would be needed to make these changes internally and then to expose existing clients to them when ready?
5. What is the overall budget for the firm to integrate online legal service delivery?
6. Who will have access to the online legal services besides the lawyers and online clients? Does the firm need a permissions-based system to allow in other parties to review and work on online matters?

What do your clients want? What do they need?

After the firm has evaluated its existing services and rebundled those services that might be most appropriate to deliver online, the firm must consider its client base and which clients would be the most receptive to the online delivery of their services. Online delivery will not be appropriate for all clients or all legal matters. For example, if a firm works largely in the area of elder law where most of the clients are perhaps not as experienced with the use of technology, such as video conferencing or logging into a client portal, this practice area may not find success with an online option for delivery. Likewise, if a law firm handles criminal defense cases or complex child custody matters, these issues are good examples where portions of the matter might be made more cost-effective through the use of a client portal and online delivery tools. However, the nature of the legal matter may require continuous and ongoing representation that would not serve the best interests of the client to be unbundled and delivered online. This step in the process of analyzing the addition of online services requires the firm to really understand its clients' needs and what would best serve them.

In addition to understanding what the client needs in online legal services, the firm may want to poll its clients to determine what online services they want. Do clients prefer to view their billing accounts and invoices online or are they more interested in using a client portal to get updates on the status of their legal matter? Would they be interested in video conferencing with lawyers in the firm or are they more comfortable with real time chat and text-based messages in a discussion board within their online account? Depending on the sophistication of the law firm's clients, their desired methods of communication and receipt of online services may be very different from law firm to law firm and from practice area to practice area. Even if a law firm gets to this stage in the process and determines that it will not be feasible to do a great deal of online legal service delivery based on its legal service offering, this exercise of understanding its clients' needs and wants in terms of traditional or online delivery will provide the firm with a useful knowledge base from which to improve its customer service practices.

The law firm may also want to consider a new target market of clients that it currently does not serve. For example, the firm may wish to provide more bespoke, full services to its sophisticated clients, but may also realize that it has the resources available to provide basic legal services in another practice area that could be packaged and commoditized through online delivery. The firm may wish to establish a very different online client base focused on those unbundled legal services. Existing, full service clients may wish to access the management of their case using the client portal, such as handling online payments and checking the status of the matter, but this will be different than the completely online client who will rely on the client portal as the sole point of access to the law firm and delivery mechanism. If a firm decides to serve clients this way, it will need to understand the different needs and desires of each target client base and expect that there may be differences in the client development and methods of working with both. This will be based on a number of factors, such as income and education level and the general nature of online clients, which tends to be more "do it yourself" than requiring the handholding of a traditional full service client. The law firm serving the needs of both types of client will want to create different procedures and processes for working with each type ahead of offering these services.

Along with understanding its clients' needs and their reception to online services, the law firm should also gauge the local courts and administrative bodies for their acceptance of online services delivered to clients. For example, if a client receives a legal form online from the law firm with instructions for filing at the courthouse, will the court assist the self-help client in the filing process or require that the barrister be present or file the document personally? The local courthouse or administration may also have restrictions on the use of technology to complete certain tasks in the judicial process. Law firms considering online legal services need to be aware of not only how online services would affect their operations, but also how the services would be received by the public, clients, the judicial system, and others in the profession.

Pricing models

Adding online legal services to a law firm may also require the restructuring of the firm's pricing model to take into consideration the cost savings of using technology to work with clients online. Depending on the level of technology used and the services delivered online, the law firm may be able to produce traditional legal services in often half the amount of time it would take without the use of cloud-based technology. The cost savings that occur with this efficiency should be passed on to the client as reduced legal fees. Additionally, many of the legal services that will be delivered online will be unbundled. Unbundled services lend themselves well to fixed or flat fee prices. If the firm is packaging a bundle of services for clients, it may be easier for the client to understand and budget for a fixed fee for that package rather than to try to guess what the law firm's traditional billable hour might be for the work. In order to determine what prices for online legal services the marketplace will bear, the law firm should go through the following suggested process.

Determine which services make sense for fixed fee prices

These will be services that are easily bundled or packaged and may be delivered almost entirely online. These will be services that the firm will have a decent idea ahead of time how long it will take, using the technology, to complete the work. If the matter has some element of complexity or the unknown to the lawyer, then it may not be the best candidate for fixed fees because it would not be possible to estimate how much time, energy, or resources would be expended by the firm in completing it.

Research competitor prices

Research the prices of online legal services provided by direct competitors. This includes pricing from non-lawyer owned legal services companies as well as law firms.

Calculate cost savings

Determine the cost savings for the firm by delivering the services online rather than with a traditional method. For example, the use of technology allows the law firm to save on average two hours' worth of associate and staff time working with a single client on a certain process.

Determine profitability

Determine how many hours the process will take. Then convert it into billable hours and see if the time spent and fixed legal fee will still amount to a billable hour rate that makes it profitable for the firm to maintain.

Identify the appropriate fixed fee

Balance this fixed fee with the prices offered by competitors. Account for the added value of the law firm's individual expertise. The correct range for the fixed fee should fall somewhere in the middle.

When a firm first begins setting fixed fees for online services, it will need to evaluate the reception of both clients and prospective clients to those rates in the larger legal marketplace. It will also have to balance the revenue coming in through the online clients with any traditional clients who may be under a different billing method, such as the billable hour or contingency fees. Analysis of the effectiveness of the prices will result in small adjustments over time as the firm determines what prices for its online services the legal marketplace will bear.

Another pricing issue that may arise for traditional firms with in-person clients may occur when those clients see the fixed fee pricing for online services and question the different pricing models. It may be necessary for a law firm to explain to its clients the difference between unbundled services delivered online and full service offerings by the firm. It may also be possible to charge a client both the traditional fees for full service while putting them on fixed fees for unbundled or packaged services that they obtain online from the law firm.

Creating the client portal

After determining the needs of the firm and its clients and selecting the appropriate technology and systems to accomplish those goals, the law firm should begin with the basic setup of the client portal. This is a simple process of working with the firm's website developer to insert a login or register feature on the existing home page of the law firm's website. The website developer is provided with the secure URL from the chosen technology vendor, which routes the individual out to the secure site where access is hosted by that third party. This URL is embedded into the image on the firm's homepage, which indicates that an existing client should "login" to their account or a new user should "register" for access.

While this basic setup is relatively simple to add to an existing law firm website, the firm should also consider revising its website design and layout to facilitate the marketing and access of the online legal services it intends to offer. For example, prospective clients may benefit from watching a short five minute tutorial video that explains the firm's online legal services or how to register for an account and request legal assistance. The firm may wish to create a separate page in the organizational structure of the website that relates only to the online legal services. This page might list the online services offered, fixed fees for those services, and an explanation of the online process of working with the firm. In terms of using online delivery as a marketing strategy for a law firm, redesigning or adjusting the firm's existing website design to reflect these additional services would help to increase the search engine optimization (SEO) for the firm's site, which drives online traffic to the firm from search engines. If a lawyer is creating a new practice from scratch and does not have a website, they would be advised to work with the website developer to create a site that prominently features the online legal services in the design.

Once the client portal has been set up on the website, the law firm should provide its existing clients with notice of account access. Depending on the technology solution the firm has chosen it may be possible to create accounts and pre-populate them with the clients' existing files prior to giving clients notice of the online services. This will take some time and significant support from members of the firm to pre-populate these accounts by importing existing contact information and the documents and files the firm wants to share with the client in their account. Another method of providing clients with access to the client portal might be to provide them with an email invitation to register for access. This email could provide an explanation of why the firm is offering these additional services and invite the client to register for access. The client may then have the choice of whether or not to do so for themselves; later in the process of working with the client, if they have not registered for access, the law firm may manually assist them in setting up the online access if desired for their case. The method of importing existing clients and/or inviting them into the client portal access will depend on the technology solution that the firm has chosen to use or has built as a custom solution for the firm.

The firm will also need to create and add the Terms of Use for the website, which includes the use of the client portal. This needs to be a static notice on the homepage of the website and accessible to anyone at any time who may be using the site. The firm's privacy policy and any other disclaimers should be referenced in the Terms of Use and also included in static form at the bottom of the home page along with the firm's contact information. These items should be dated so that the user is aware of when they were drafted and last updated. In addition to the static Terms of Use, the registration process for the client portal should require that the prospective client reviews a clickwrap agreement that lays out the terms of use for the online legal services. This document might include such items as an explanation of the nature of unbundled legal services, the methods of online communication, the firm's social media policy, the storage and return of client data in digital format, etc. Additionally, the technology vendor chosen by the law firm may include sample language for use in the registration process. Once the law firm decides to establish the lawyer-client relationship for online legal service delivery, the firm will send, through the client portal, a more specific limited scope engagement agreement detailing the exact scope of the services to be delivered online. However, for the prospective client registering to request legal assistance prior to working with the firm, the clickwrap language needs to be in the registration process for the client portal. This protects the law firm in terms of its duties to prospective clients.

This first appeared as Chapter 1 in Kimbro, S., Online Legal Services for the Client-Centric Law Firm, *Ark Group, 2013.*

About the author

Stephanie Kimbro, MA, JD is a fellow at Stanford Law School with the Center on the Legal Profession. She is also the co-director of the Center for Law Practice Technology. She is the recipient of the 2009 ABA Keane Award for Excellence in eLawyering and, in addition to *Online Legal Services for the Client-Centric Law Firm*, she is the author of *Virtual Law Practice: How to Deliver Legal Services Online* (2010), *Limited Scope Legal Services: Unbundling and the Self-Help Client* (2012), and *The Consumer Law Revolution: The Lawyers' Guide to the Online Legal Marketplace* (2013), all published by the American Bar Association. She is also the co-founder of Virtual Law Office Technology, LLC (VLOTech), which was acquired by Total Attorneys in the fall of 2009.

In addition to practicing law, Stephanie writes about the ethics and technology issues of delivering legal services online and is interested in the use of technology to increase access to justice. She has provided presentations and guest lectured for many state bars, law schools, and other organizations interested in legal technology. She authors a blog about the online delivery of legal services at www.virtuallawpractice.org.

Stephanie is an adjunct professor at several law schools and is currently developing two mobile games for legal services, including one related to eviction law for Illinois Legal Aid Online, through her new venture, Game on Law, L3C.

Reference

1. ABA Legal Technology Survey Report, May 2013, available at: http://apps.americanbar.org/abastore/index.cfm?section=main&fm=Product.AddToCart&pid=2680130PDF.

www.ingramcontent.com/pod-product-compliance
Ingram Content Group UK Ltd.
Pitfield, Milton Keynes, MK11 3LW, UK
UKHW050231160926
8657IPUK00008B/193

9 781783 581795